# FINDING
# PEACE
# WORKBOOK

### GOD'S PROMISE OF A LIFE FREE
### FROM REGRET, ANXIETY, AND FEAR

# CHARLES F. STANLEY

OLIVER
NELSON

THOMAS NELSON PUBLISHERS®
Nashville

A Division of Thomas Nelson, Inc.
www.ThomasNelson.com

Published in Nashville, Tennessee, by Thomas Nelson, Inc.

ISBN: 0-7852-6184-2

*Printed in the United States of America*

03 04 05 06 07 VG 5 4 3 2 1

# CONTENTS

INTRODUCTION

# GETTING THE MOST OUT OF THE
# *FINDING PEACE WORKBOOK*

## A WORD FROM
## DR. CHARLES STANLEY

At the very outset of this workbook, I want to call your attention to several features that I believe will be very helpful to you in your study. In fact, they are the features that are at the very heart of this workbook.

This workbook is intended to accompany the book titled *Finding Peace* (Thomas Nelson Publishers 2003). You will see references to *Finding Peace* from time to time, along with the page numbers from that book which I have referenced in this workbook.

There are four features that are repeated frequently in this workbook.

## KEY FEATURE 1:
## REFLECT AND RESPOND

One of the great ways of studying God's Word is to sit and read a passage of God's Word, and then pause to reflect upon what that passage really says.

As part of the *Reflection and Response* sections, you are going to be asked to respond to verses from the Bible that relate to a particular topic. You will see the words *General response* and *Personal response*.

The phrase *General response* is my challenge to you to find the key concept in the verse or passage—the central meaning that applies to all people, all the time.

The phrase *Personal response* is my challenge to you to state what you believe God is saying to you very personally. God's personal word to you is very directional and concrete—it is the applying of the verse to people, places, things, and situations you are facing.

*You will find a sample of how to do this in the Appendix to this workbook.*

I encourage you to allow the truth of God's Word to sink deep into your soul. Let it nourish you, build you up, change you, and mold you into the person God wants you to be.

## TO SHARE OR NOT TO SHARE

Not everything that you reflect about, and certainly not all of your responses, should necessarily be made public.

This workbook can certainly be used for group discussions or a small-group Bible study. In fact, I encourage you to get involved in group Bible study and to talk over some of the concepts of this book with other people. There's great benefit in hearing the experiences and insights of other people.

But *all* that you write in *Reflection and Response* need not be shared. Those things that are part of your *Personal response* in many cases should be kept private. Otherwise, you simply won't be as honest and your responses won't be complete.

So what should be discussed and what shouldn't be discussed? Look for this symbol and heading:

### DISCUSSION POINT

The questions or ideas that have this symbol and heading are especially good for personal meditation and reflection and group discussion.

## KEY FEATURE 2:
## A LETTER TO GOD

Many years ago I developed a practice that has proven to be highly valuable to me through countless situations, heartaches, and challenges. I began to write letters to God.

At times my letter was filled with statements that were marked by anguish, hurt, or pain. Sometimes my letter was a statement that allowed me to vent very deep frustrations, disappointments, or concerns. Sometimes it would be a place for me to identify questions I had—along with a plea for God's answers. Sometimes my letters were a way for me to tell God about my worries and fears.

Some of my letters were fairly short. Others were very long.

Two of the greatest things about these letters is that they were and continue to be very honest and very personal.

There's no point in writing a letter to God if it isn't totally, brutally, and completely honest. Who are you trying to kid? God knows what's lurking in your heart and mind. He knows what is troubling you. The benefit of your expressing yourself so honestly and fully to God is not to inform God about something. The benefit is so you can reread what you have written and inform *yourself* about what it is that you are truly thinking and feeling.

*You can see an example of one young woman's letter to God in the Appendix to this workbook.* Her fiancé had been killed in an auto accident, and she allowed me to print her letter to God so that others might be helped by reading it.

*A Letter to God* has these two rules:

1. Get it all out before God.

2. Keep it all private from other people.

## KEY FEATURE 3:
## THANKS-AND-PRAISE LISTS

What can we do to turn ourselves away from a negative situation or condition and toward a positive state of peace? The answer is one type of prayer: thanksgiving and praise.

Thanksgiving focuses on the blessings we have received from God—all of the positive things we have experienced or are experiencing.

Praise focuses us on the Giver of all blessings—it points us toward the attributes and nature of God, which is 100 percent positive all the time!

We are wise, then, when we are troubled, or when we find ourselves in negative or disturbing situations and conditions, to begin to praise and thank God.

From time to time in this workbook I will challenge you to make a "Thanksgiving and Praise List." Be creative in making your lists. List things that are highly concrete and specific, and things that are abstract and more general. For example, you might thank God for "a family who loves me," "beauty," "the light through my kitchen window," "answers," and "for seeing two beautiful butterflies in my yard." Nothing is too great or too small for thanksgiving!

The same holds true for your praise. So often we repeat the phrase "Praise God" over and over and never mention any aspect of His nature in our praise. Praise God for being your Savior, your Healer, your Deliverer, your Sure Foundation. Praise God for His glory, His majesty, His splendor, His power, His love, His tender care, His leading and guidance, and His willingness to protect and provide.

## KEY FEATURE 4:
## FILING A GRIEVANCE STATEMENT

All of us know what it means to hold a grudge—a feeling of resentment, bitterness, anger, or even hatred.

A grievance statement is a very straightforward statement about what you think a person did to you that hurt you in any way.

Start your grievance statement this way: "I have a grievance against you, _____ _____ (fill in the person's name)."

A grievance statement very often continues with one of these phrases:

"I felt great hurt or pain when you . . ."
"I felt deep disappointment when you . . ."
"I am very angry at you for . . ."

The point is not simply to write out a grievance statement, but then to submit that statement to the Lord Jesus. It is to hold this statement before the Lord and say, "Jesus, You see how I feel. You see what this person did to me. You see how my life has been impacted by this and how much anguish I've been living with. I give this grievance statement to You. Please deal with this person who has trespassed on my life and caused me offense. Please deal with me too—heal me, restore me, help me to move from pain to wholeness, from shame to forgiveness. Please free me from these memories so I might hold my head high and walk forward into my future with boldness, strength, and renewed energy."

---

This brief introduction to the *Finding Peace Workbook* is all you need to get started. However, if you would like to go even deeper into the material in this workbook, in the Appendix I have written a guided explanation of each section. You will find more detailed instructions if you need them, and you'll see examples of each element.

# ONE

# WHO'S IN CONTROL?

## TOTAL ASSURANCE ABOUT WHO IS IN CONTROL

Long ago I came to the total assurance that God loves me, God knows where I am every second of every day, and God is bigger than any problem life's circumstances can throw at me. I have complete confidence that God is able to take care of any situation and provide an answer to any question or problem—He has all the resources of the universe to draw upon in helping each one of us through any type of crisis if we will trust Him.

Based upon many challenging events in my life, I *know* with deep certainty that God is *always* in control. He will never leave me, turn His back on me, reject me, or withdraw His love from me. He delights in showing me again and again that He is the source of my strength, my provision, my protection, and my ultimate success in life. I have absolutely no doubt that God is in control of every second of my future. (From *Finding Peace*, pages 5–6)

### REFLECTION AND RESPONSE

Quickly answer the questions below. Give the answer that spontaneously comes to your mind—not the answer you think may be right or the answer you have after prayerful reflection:

Who is in control of your life? (A spouse? A parent? An institution or government agency? A supervisor at work?) List every influence, power, or authority that you believe is in control of some aspect of your life:

_____

_____

_____

_____

_____

Who is in control of your *future*?

_____

_____

Now let me ask you an even more important question: Who is ultimately in control of the people or institutions that you believe are in control of your life and future?

_____

In the paragraphs above from *Finding Peace*, I made several statements that I consider to reflect absolutes in my life. Some of those statements are repeated below. What is your response?

|  | I'D LIKE TO BELIEVE THIS, BUT I REALLY DON'T | I THINK THIS MAY BE TRUE SOMETIMES | I BELIEVE THIS IS TRUE ALL THE TIME—NO DOUBT! |
|---|---|---|---|
| 1. God loves me. | _____ | _____ | _____ |
| 2. God knows where I am every second of every day. | _____ | _____ | _____ |
| 3. God is bigger than any problem life's circumstances can throw at me. | _____ | _____ | _____ |
| 4. God will never leave me, turn His back on me, reject me, or withdraw His love from me. | _____ | _____ | _____ |
| 5. I have absolutely no doubt that God is in control of every second of my future. | _____ | _____ | _____ |

## WHAT ARE YOUR "ISSUES" WITH GOD?

Many people find that they have an *issue* with God—in today's use of that word, an *issue* is having some sort of trouble in accepting the nature of God and the relationship He desires to have with a person. I believe these are the three foremost issues people have: a *love* issue, a *capability* issue, and a *freewill* issue.

### THE LOVE ISSUE

These are classic statements from people who have trouble accepting that God loves them:

- God is judgmental and unloving.
- God may love mankind in general, but He doesn't love me personally and individually.

What do you believe?

_____

_____

_____

_____

∞

*Reflect upon and then respond to the verses below in both* general *and* personal *ways. Indicate what you believe to be the general message of these passages, and then identify what you believe the Lord has as a personal message to you.*

1 JOHN 4:9–10~In this the love of God was manifested toward us, that God has sent His only begotten Son into the world, that we might live through Him. In this is love, not that we loved God, but that He loved us and sent His Son to be the propitiation for our sins.

*General response:*

_____

_____

_____

_____

*Personal response:*

_____

_____

_____

_____

1 JOHN 4:15–16~Whoever confesses that Jesus is the Son of God, God abides in him, and he in God. And we have known and believed the love that God has for us. God is love, and he who abides in love abides in God, and God in him.

*General response:*

_____

_____

_____

_____

*Personal response:*

_____

_____

_____

_____

## THE CAPABILITY ISSUE

People who have this difficulty with God tend to make statements such as these:

• God set up the universe, but He's left it up to us human beings to manage it.

• God is in control in general terms, but He couldn't possibly be in control of all the details of each one of our lives.

What do you believe?

_____

_____

_____

_____

_____


MATTHEW 6:13~For Yours is the kingdom and the power and the glory forever. (This is part of the Lord's Prayer.)

*General response:*

_____

_____

_____

_____

_____


*Personal response:*

_____

_____

_____

_____


PSALM 71:5–6~For You are my hope, O Lord GOD; You are my trust from my youth. By You I have been upheld from birth; You are He who took me out of my mother's womb. My praise shall be continually of You.

*General response:*

_____

_____

_____

_____

*Personal response:*

_____

_____

_____

_____

## THE FREEWILL ISSUE

Those who have trouble with God when it comes to the issue of free will often make statements such as these:

- God is in control of my life only to the extent that I give Him control.

- God never overrides free will and therefore He can't fully control others who may have control over my life in some area, especially those who aren't in relationship with Him.

What do you believe?

_____

_____

_____

_____

*Reflect upon and then respond to the verses below in both* general *and* personal *ways. Indicate what you believe to be the general message of these passages, and then identify what you believe the Lord has as a personal message to you.*

PSALM 81:11–14~My people would not heed My voice,

And Israel would have none of Me.

So I gave them over to their own stubborn heart,

To walk in their own counsels.

Oh, that My people would listen to Me,

That Israel would walk in My ways!

I would soon subdue their enemies,

And turn My hand against their adversaries.

*General response:*

_____

_____

_____

*Personal response:*

_____

_____

_____

MARK 14:36~[Jesus] said, "Abba, Father, all things are possible for You. Take this cup away from Me; nevertheless, not what I will, but what You will."

*General response:*

_____

_____

_____

_____

*Personal response:*

_____

_____

_____

_____

_____

## THE ISSUE OF CONTROL IS VITAL TO OUR LIVES

If you are controlled by the particular situation you are facing, you can't have peace, because at any second that situation can spin out of control. Life's circumstances can change in a heartbeat.

If some evil power is in control, you're certainly in trouble.

If another person controls you or the circumstance in which you are involved, you may have peace for a while, but eventually that person may disappoint you and let you down in some way, and then you can lose your peace.

If you are in control, you may appear to have the power to guarantee yourself a peaceful existence, but eventually you are going to make a mistake or something/someone will enter the picture to rearrange your circumstances, and before you know it, boom! Trouble with a capital *T* is at your door, and then you will find that your ability to create and control your own serenity was a mere illusion.

But what if God is in control of your life? With Him steering the ship, there's every reason to hope, every reason to feel confident, and every reason to move forward boldly in your life, expecting the best out of every experience. (From *Finding Peace*, pages 6–7)

### REFLECTION AND RESPONSE

Some people seem to believe that nobody is in control—that this universe is spinning out of control and everything happens according to random chance.

Consider the fact that the earth is moving in at least six different ways simultaneously, yet we are not dizzy.

1. The earth spins on its axis like a top, at the speed of ⅙ mile per second or 1,000 miles per hour.

2. The earth weaves slowly back and forth on its axis, tilting to an angle of

23 degrees, then swinging slowly back. It does this twice a year, giving us our seasons.

3. The earth, with the moon, is swinging around the sun once a year at a rate of 18½ miles per second. It never varies $\frac{1}{100,000}$ of a second on this annual trip.

4. The sun, with all its planets, is on a trip, rushing northward at 12 miles per second.

5. The nearby stars, with our planetary system, are revolving at 180 miles per second around the Milky Way's center.

6. The Milky Way, our galaxy, with all its millions of stars, is on a tremendous journey, plunging through space at terrific speeds. Nobody has been able to determine if this is movement toward a destination or is an orbit.

Now consider your own heart. It beats an average of 75 times a minute, forty million times a year, or two and a half billion times in seventy years. At each beat, the average adult heart discharges about four ounces of blood. This amounts to 3,000 gallons a day or 650,000 gallons a year. That's enough to fill more than 81 tank cars of a railway train.

The heart does enough work in one hour to lift a 150-pound man to the top of a three-story building, enough energy in 12 hours to lift a 65-ton tank car one foot off the ground, or enough power in 70 years to lift the largest battleship afloat completely out of the water.

Who is in control?

---

## Discussion Point

What other examples have you heard about or encountered that lead you to conclude that Almighty God is not only our Creator but the One who remains in total control of our lives every second of our existence?

---

---

_____

_____

∞

## THANKS AND PRAISE

The automatic response to our God who is always, always, *always* in control of our lives must surely be thanksgiving and praise. Make a list of at least ten things that you are thankful for today—focus on those aspects of God's love, capability, and control.

_____

_____

_____

_____

_____

_____

_____

_____

_____

_____

❧

# TWO

# THE FOUNDATION FOR ALL PEACE

## THE GOD OF PEACE DESIRES
## A RELATIONSHIP WITH YOU

The God who controls all things, who is present in your life, whether you acknowledge Him or not, is the God of Peace. That is the meaning of His name—Jehovah Shalom, the God of Peace—and He has done a marvelous thing in creating this world and all the elements in it. He has purposely designed it with a plan in mind. And that plan includes *you!*

Therein lies the problem. If you are unaware that there is a plan or that you are part of that plan, then you will be unable to recognize His signposts along the way. What so many sense as their "loneliness" and others as a "deep void" or "purposelessness" is, in actuality, one of the signals that God has placed within us. It is His programmed message that we need Him. The designer is telling His creation, "Without Me you will never feel complete. I am the only One who can satisfy your deep-seated longings. I will be the source of your peace." (From *Finding Peace*, pages 11–12)

### REFLECTION AND RESPONSE

Gideon, a great leader in the history of Israel, was the first person in the Bible to refer to God as "Jehovah Shalom"—the God of Peace. Gideon, however, did not live in a peaceful time. Nor was he a peaceful man at the outset of his story. The Bible tells us in Judges 6 that the children of Israel had sinned in God's eyes and the Lord had delivered them into the hands of the Midianites for seven years. These were terrible years—the Midianites stripped the land of all produce and animals to the point that the entire nation was greatly impoverished. The people of Israel were so frightened of these invaders that they made their homes in caves, dens, and strongholds in the mountains. The nation was "hiding out" with what little provision remained.

God sent a prophet to the children of Israel but nobody responded to his message. Then the Angel of the Lord came to Gideon, who was threshing wheat in a winepress in order to hide the grain from the Midianites. Now read about what happened next.

∞

*Reflect upon and then respond to the verses below in both* general *and* personal *ways. Indicate what you believe to be the general message of these passages, and then identify what you believe the Lord has as a personal message to you.*

JUDGES 6:12–24~And the Angel of the LORD appeared to [Gideon], and said to him, "The LORD is with you, you mighty man of valor!"

Gideon said to Him, "O my lord, if the LORD is with us, why then has all this happened to us? And where are all His miracles which our fathers told us about, saying, 'Did not the LORD bring us up from Egypt?' But now the LORD has forsaken us and delivered us into the hands of the Midianites."

Then the LORD turned to him and said, "Go in this might of yours, and you shall save Israel from the hand of the Midianites. Have I not sent you?"

So he said to Him, "O my LORD, how can I save Israel? Indeed my clan is the weakest in Manasseh, and I am the least in my father's house."

And the LORD said to him, "Surely I will be with you, and you shall defeat the Midianites as one man."

Then he said to Him, "If now I have found favor in Your sight, then show me a sign that it is You who talk with me. Do not depart from here, I pray, until I come to You and bring out my offering and set it before You."

And He said, "I will wait until you come back."

So Gideon went in and prepared a young goat, and unleavened bread from an ephah of flour. The meat he put in a basket, and he put the broth in a pot; and he brought them out to Him under the terebinth tree and presented them. The Angel of God said to him, "Take the meat and the unleavened bread and lay them on this rock, and pour out the broth." And he did so.

Then the Angel of the LORD put out the end of the staff that was in His hand, and touched the meat and the unleavened bread; and fire rose out of the rock and consumed the meat and the unleavened bread. And the Angel of the LORD departed out of his sight.

Now Gideon perceived that He was the Angel of the LORD. So Gideon said, "Alas, O Lord GOD! For I have seen the Angel of the LORD face to face."

Then the LORD said to him, "Peace be with you; do not fear, you shall not die." So Gideon built an altar there to the LORD, and called it The-LORD-Is-Peace.

∾

## DISCUSSION POINT

Have you ever blamed God for a situation in your life that you might describe as "unpeaceful"?

_____

_____

_____

_____

Has the Lord ever asked you to do something that you felt totally unworthy or incapable of doing? Did you feel peaceful at that time, even though you may have felt with certainty that God was calling you to a particular task or mission?

_____

_____

_____

How would you have felt if your offering of bread, meat, and broth was totally consumed by fire and then the angel that had appeared to you disappeared from your sight? Would you have felt peaceful?

_____

_____

_____

_____

If you had grown up believing, as Gideon had, that any person who saw God face-to-face died immediately, would you have felt peaceful after realizing you had spoken to God face-to-face?

_____

_____

_____

_____

In the light of all his lack of peace, why did Gideon build an altar to Jehovah-Shalom—The-Lord-Is-Peace? What difference did it make that the Lord *spoke* to him, "Peace be with you; do not fear; you shall not die"? What are the most comforting words the Lord might speak to your heart today? Aren't they the same words in the context of your experiencing eternal life?

_____

_____

_____

_____

Luke 2:8–10~Now there were in the same country shepherds living out in the fields, keeping watch over their flock by night. And behold, an angel of the Lord stood before them, and the glory of the Lord shone around them, and they were greatly afraid. Then the angel said to them, "Do not be afraid, for behold, I bring you good tidings of great joy which will be to all people."

*General response:*

_____

_____

_____

_____

_____

*Personal response:*

_____

_____

_____

_____

JOHN 14:1~[Jesus said]: "Let not your heart be troubled; you believe in God, believe also in Me."

*General response:*

_____

_____

_____

_____

*Personal response:*

_____

_____

_____

_____

Do you believe you are at peace today with God? Is the Lord truly "Peace" (Jehovah-Shalom) to you? Why or why not?

_____

_____

_____

_____

_____

## YOUR STATUS WITH GOD

God's plan was to create mankind so that we would have a relationship with Him. This relationship would be characterized by love: God's loving us and our loving Him. And through His loving presence, He would protect and provide for us. This idea was and is unique to Judeo-Christian religious thought.

No matter what other relationships we share, what our status is in life, where we have been and what we have done on our life journeys, God designed us to have this intimate relationship with Himself. He knew that out of this intimacy of relationship we could receive His gift to all who follow Him—a deep, lasting, abiding peace that only He can provide to the human heart.

For some of you, however, there is a fundamental problem with this plan. You may never have heard about it, or perhaps you may never have had someone explain it to you in a clear way. Then again, you may have rejected the plan in earlier years for whatever reason, and you now sense deep inside the ongoing emptiness. You know *now* is the time for you to find the answer to your need. (From *Finding Peace*, pages 12–13)

### REFLECTION AND RESPONSE

Have you accepted Jesus as your Savior? That is ultimately God's plan for *you*. Reflect on the well-known verse below. What new insights do you have into God's plan, not only for the whole world but *for your life?*

JOHN 3:16–17~For God so loved the world that He gave His only begotten Son, that whoever believes in Him should not perish but have everlasting life. For God did not send His Son into the world to condemn the world, but that the world through Him might be saved.

*General response:*

_____

_____

_____

_____

*Personal response:*

_____

_____

_____

_____

Sin causes us to become more and more self-centered and to drift farther and farther away from God and His plan. Then, when we are faced with pain, suffering, loneliness, estrangement, or death, we are unable to cope. We don't have the inner resources to bring peace to our troubled hearts. Our souls have become bankrupt. God's desire is to bring us back into right relationship with Him.

Is that the desire of your heart?

## A Letter to God

If your desire today is to turn from your sin and to receive Jesus as your Savior, I invite you to write a letter to God about this.

Perhaps you have already accepted Jesus as your Savior. If your desire today is to renew your relationship with God, use this opportunity to write a letter to God telling Him how thankful you are for your salvation, how much you love Him, and how you desire to renew relationship with Him.

Let God know how you have felt about Him in the past—or how you feel about Him right now. What have you thought about Him—in other words, what was your opinion of Him? Be honest with yourself and honest with God today.

Admit your sins to Him. Acknowledge your rebellion against His plan. If you simply haven't known His plan before now, tell Him that. Admit that you are in need of a Savior.

Then express to God that you are sorry for your sins and ask Him to forgive you. Ask Him to give you a new heart, a new life, and a new future—an everlasting future. Even if you are already a Christian, there's always room for repentance, confession of those things you have done or failed to do, and a renewal of your commitment to serve God with your whole heart, mind, and soul.

# JESUS IS THE FOUNDATION STONE

Jesus is the foundation stone of our peace. He bridges the gap between God and man. The Scriptures say, "He is our peace." And what wonderful benefits are ours: forgiveness (no more shame or guilt because of the past), the continuous assurance of God's presence in our lives, and more to the point of this book, *His peace*—the gift that is given to those who begin to follow the Master. (From *Finding Peace*, pages 16–17)

## REFLECTION AND RESPONSE

Take a few minutes to reflect and respond to the three great benefits that come with our acceptance of Christ—forgiveness (no more shame or guilt because of the past), the assurance of God's presence, and God's peace.

## THE GIFT OF GOD'S FORGIVENESS

1 JOHN 1:9~If we confess our sins, He is faithful and just to forgive us our sins and to cleanse us from all unrighteousness.

*General response:*

_____

_____

_____

_____

*Personal response:*

_____

_____

_____

_____

ROMANS 10:9–13~If you confess with your mouth the Lord Jesus and believe in your heart that God has raised Him from the dead, you will be saved. For with the heart one believes unto righteousness, and with the mouth confession is made unto salvation. For the Scripture says, "Whoever believes on Him will not be put to shame." For there is no distinction between Jew and Greek, for the same Lord over all is rich to all who call upon Him. For "whoever calls on the name of the LORD shall be saved."

*General response:*

_____

_____

_____

_____

*Personal response:*

_____

_____

_____

_____

## THE GIFT OF GOD'S PRESENCE

MATTHEW 28:18–20~Jesus came and spoke to them, saying, "All authority has been given to Me in heaven and on earth. Go therefore and make disciples of all the nations, baptizing them in the name of the Father and of the Son and of the Holy Spirit, teaching them to observe all things that I have commanded you; and lo, I am with you always, even to the end of the age."

*General response:*

_____

_____

_____

_____

*Personal response:*

_____

_____

_____

JOHN 14:16–18~I will pray the Father, and He will give you another Helper, that He may abide with you forever—the Spirit of truth, whom the world cannot receive, because it neither sees Him nor knows Him; but you know Him, for He dwells with you and will be in you. I will not leave you orphans; I will come to you.

*General response:*

_____

_____

_____

_____

*Personal response:*

_____

_____

_____

_____

## THE GIFT OF GOD'S PEACE

JOHN 16:33~These things I have spoken to you, that in Me you may have peace. In the world you will have tribulation; but be of good cheer, I have overcome the world.

*General response:*

_____

_____

_____

_____

*Personal response:*

_____

_____

_____

_____

## DISCUSSION POINT

Do you tend to experience greater peace if you know in *advance* of a possible negative situation what you might expect or anticipate?

_____

_____

Do you tend to experience greater peace if you know the purpose for why something negative is happening?

_____

_____

## THANKS AND PRAISE

The most important event of your life is your acceptance of Jesus as your Savior. There is no greater cause for thanksgiving or for praise. Identify below at least ten things for which you are grateful—focus on those things that are related to your salvation and to your receiving God's great gifts of forgiveness and eternal life. Offer thanks and praise, also, for God's promise of His unbroken and unwavering presence and love, and for His peace.

_____

_____

_____

_____

_____

_____

_____

_____

_____

_____

_____

_____

_____

_____

# THREE

❦

# THE QUALITY OF PEACE GOD GIVES

## THE WORLD'S PEACE AND GOD'S PEACE

Even the most happy and contented person, over the course of his or her life, often grudgingly admits that something is missing. The humble follower of Jesus knows that the essential ingredient for all persons to be happy, contented, and at peace within themselves is the presence of God.

Remember, what the world offers as "peace" is ultimately an illusion, even though it may appear very concrete. It is like a mirage in the desert. A mirage looks like a body of water. But in fact, it does not exist and therefore is never attainable. A mirage has absolutely no ability to quench thirst.

The world regards peace as being the by-product of doing the right deeds, saying the right words, working in the right job, or having the right intentions.

That isn't at all the criteria for peace described in God's Word. Peace is an inner quality that flows out of a right relationship with God. (From *Finding Peace*, page 22)

### REFLECTION AND RESPONSE

One of the most famous passages of the Bible is Psalm 23. It is frequently memorized and often quoted. Are you aware, however, that this psalm likely was written while David was "on the run" from a jealous and angry King Saul, who was attempting to kill him? David likely wrote this psalm while he was in "hiding." Not only was his life at stake, but the lives of several hundred men who had banded together with him. One could hardly describe David's situation as happy, contented, or "living a life of peace."

With this context in mind, reflect upon this psalm and respond to it. Circle or underline words or phrases that have special meaning to you.

PSALM 23 ~The LORD is my shepherd; I shall not want.

        He makes me to lie down in green pastures;

        He leads me beside the still waters.

        He restores my soul;

        He leads me in the paths of righteousness

        For His name's sake.

        Yea, though I walk through the valley of the shadow of death,

        I will fear no evil;

        For You are with me;

        Your rod and Your staff, they comfort me.

        You prepare a table before me in the presence of my enemies;

        You anoint my head with oil;

        My cup runs over.

        Surely goodness and mercy shall follow me

        All the days of my life;

        And I will dwell in the house of the LORD

        Forever.

*General response:*

_____

_____

_____

_____

*Personal response:*

_____

_____

_____

_____

## THE WORLD'S PEACE

What do you believe has been taught to you by the world as necessary for you to experience peace? Make a list of several things that are equated with peace.

_____

_____

_____

_____

_____

_____

Now, go back over that list and put an *X* beside every item that you personally have believed to be necessary for peace. Be honest with yourself! (If you believe good health or having five hundred dollars in your wallet is necessary for you to feel peace, say so!)

Are these items that David had as he lived in a wilderness area, hiding out in order to stay alive?

_____

_____

❧

### Discussion Point

On what did David rely for peace since he did not likely have the material wealth, social acceptability and mobility, or comfortable living conditions so often equated with peace by the world?

## GOD'S PEACE

What similar or related words do you associate with the peace God gives? In other words, how does it *feel* to you to experience God's peace? What are the qualities of God's peace, or the accompaniments to God's peace? Make a list of several words that are related to God's peace.

_____

_____

_____

_____

Now go back and put an *X* by those words that you believe you have experienced personally. What more would you like to experience as aspects of God's peace?

_____

_____

_____

_____

## DISCUSSION POINT

Can you see a marked difference in the quality of the peace the world advocates and the quality of peace God gives?

## GOD'S PEACE TRANSCENDS CIRCUMSTANCES

God's peace is not a denial of reality. God never intends for us to turn a blind eye to the reality of any situation, including evil. Rather, He intends for us to confront reality with our faith and with an abiding peace in our hearts.

Neither is God's peace an escape from reality. We are not transfixed or somehow mentally "removed" from feeling pain or struggling. Peace is not a stupor that dulls our senses. It is not an elimination of responsibility for addressing hard issues and difficult circumstances. Rather, peace is an undergirding rock-solid foundation so that no matter the tears we cry or the sorrow we feel, deep down inside we know with an abiding assurance that God is with us. God is in control, and the joy of the Lord is going to emerge far greater than any depth of agony we may be experiencing.

All of God's children go through storms in their journeys through life. It is precisely in the "going through" stage of any crisis that God's peace is most clearly manifested to all. (From *Finding Peace*, page 23)

## REFLECTION AND RESPONSE

Reflect back over your life for a moment. What has God brought you through?

Take a few minutes to recall a specific experience—perhaps the most difficult experience of your life—and note how God brought you through that difficulty. Make this very personal.

- What were the circumstances in which you found yourself?

_____

_____

_____

_____

- What did God do? How did He manifest His presence to you? What did you experience spiritually?

_____

_____

_____

_____

- Who, if anyone, did God use in your life to help you experience His peace?

_____

_____

_____

_____

- How did God minister to you—directly and through people—to bring you to a place of peace?

  _____

  _____

  _____

  _____

- From where to where did God lead you spiritually—in other words, what was the state of your soul before this experience and what was the state of your soul as you emerged from it?

  _____

  _____

  _____

  _____

Does the following verse have special meaning to you in the light of what God has brought you through in your life?

1 JOHN 4:4~He who is in you is greater than he who is in the world.

*General response:*

_____

_____

_____

_____

*Personal response:*

_____

_____

_____

_____

∞

### THANKS AND PRAISE

Have you taken time lately to offer your thanks and praise to God for the way He brought you through the experience you have recalled above? Take some time now to write your thanks and praise to God!

_____

_____

_____

_____

## GOD'S PEACE SURPASSES UNDERSTANDING

The peace God gives is something you can't necessarily figure out. You can't always under-stand how it operates in you. God doesn't intend it to be understood by the human mind or explained in a natural manner. (From *Finding Peace*, page 25)

### A Letter to God

Take time to write a letter to God about what troubles you—about life in general, yourself, your relationships, or about Him. How comfortable are you in situations where you can't figure out or anticipate what is happening? How comfortable are you experiencing God in ways that don't seem understandable by the mind? Do you have doubts or frustrations about your failure to make sense of life at times? Express to God your willingness or reluctance to experience a peace that *surpasses* understanding.

∞

_____

_____

_____

_____

_____

_____

_____

_____

_____

_____

_____

_____

_____

_____

_____

_____

_____

_____

_____

_____

_____

_____

_____

_____

_____

_____

REFLECTION AND RESPONSE

The apostle Paul had a powerful influence for the gospel during much of his life. The last few years of his life, however, Paul was in prison or under house arrest in both Caesarea (Israel) and Rome. Part of that time he was in chains, bound to Roman soldiers who were keeping guard over him. This certainly was a far cry from the times when Paul felt free to go wherever the Holy Spirit led him to travel. Even so, it was while he was in *prison* that Paul wrote to the church he had established in Philippi: "The peace of God, which surpasses all understanding, will guard your hearts and minds" (Phil. 4:7).

Take a few minutes to reflect more fully upon what Paul wrote to the Philippians. Note specific words or phrases and reflect upon their meaning to your life and perhaps to a current situation.

PHIIPPIANS. 4:1, 4–7~Stand fast in the Lord, beloved . . . Rejoice in the Lord always. Again I will say, rejoice! Let your gentleness be known to all men. The Lord is at hand. Be anxious for nothing, but in everything by prayer and supplication, with thanksgiving, let your requests be made known to God; and the peace of God, which surpasses all understanding, will guard your hearts and minds through Christ Jesus.

*General response:*

_____

_____

_____

_____

*Personal response:*

_____

_____

_____

_____

Have you ever felt this kind of peace that Paul described to the Philippians—a peace that envelops you even though, given the circumstances you are in, you should be feeling anything *but* peace? Take a few minutes to recall that experience:

• What happened? Who was involved? How did you feel?

_____

_____

_____

_____

_____

• Where were you—not only physically but spiritually—in your walk with the Lord?

_____

_____

_____

_____

_____

• How did God intervene, and what was your response to Him?

_____

_____

_____

_____

• What was the outcome of that experience in your life—not only in the natural, but also in your spiritual relationship with God? What did you learn or gain from that experience?

_____

_____

_____

_____

_____

_____

_____

## THANKS AND PRAISE

Have you taken time lately to thank and praise God for giving you His supernatural peace? Take a few minutes to write out a praise statement to the Lord!

_____

_____

_____

_____

_____

_____

_____

_____

_____

_____

_____

_____

## GOD'S PEACE IS A PROMISE

Peace is a promise of God, and as mentioned before, the promises of God are for women and men of all ages, in all cultures, in all nations, throughout all generations. God does not give promises and then take them back. He does not offer a gift and then fail to deliver it. His promise of peace is for you! (From *Finding Peace*, page 26)

## REFLECTION AND RESPONSE

∞

*Reflect upon and then respond to the verses below in both* general *and* personal *ways. Indicate what you believe to be the general message of these passages, and then identify what you believe the Lord has as a personal message to you.*

JOHN 14:27~[Jesus said:] "Peace I leave with you, My peace I give to you."

*General response:*

_____

_____

_____

_____

*Personal response:*

_____

_____

_____

_____

ROMANS 2:8–11~To those who are self-seeking and do not obey the truth, but obey unrighteousness—indignation and wrath, tribulation and anguish, on every soul of man who does evil, of the Jew first and also of the Greek; but glory, honor, and peace to everyone who works what is good, to the Jew first and also to the Greek. For there is no partiality with God.

*General response:*

_____

_____

_____

_____

_____

_____

*Personal response:*

_____

_____

_____

_____

NOTE: Is there a specific "good" that God is calling you to do?

PSALM 34:14~Depart from evil and do good;
   Seek peace and pursue it.

(As you read this verse in Psalm 34, also refer to Jesus' promise in Matthew 7:7~Seek, and you will find.)

*General response:*

_____

_____

_____

_____

_____

_____

*Personal response:*

_____

_____

_____

_____

_____

NOTE: Is there something specific God is calling you to "depart from"? Is there something specific God is calling you to "pursue"?

## GOD'S PEACE IS AN ABIDING STATE OF BEING

God's desire is that you feel an abiding peace all the time, a peace that includes joy and a feeling of purpose in every area of your life—with times of anxiety or frustration being the "spurts" that occasionally hit you in crisis moments. Plain and simple, a troubled soul is not God's desired norm for you; a heart anchored in peace is. (From *Finding Peace*, page 28)

## A Grievance Statement Against Those Who Attempt to Steal Your Peace

Ultimately, nobody can *steal* your peace. You must give up peace.

There are those who do attempt to steal your peace—who seek to destroy your reputation, damage your integrity, do you physical or financial harm, abuse you in some way, or tempt you to the point of frustration. This is the time to address the attempts made against your peace—past and present.

In writing out your grievance statement, be sure to address specific people who you believe have attempted to steal your peace. Identify why you believe these people are successful at times—in other words, why you give up your peace to the attacks of certain individuals. Also identify ways in which you have been taught erroneously—or have failed to be taught—how to confront or cope with those who attempt to steal your peace.

Finally, be sure to address the enemy of your soul—the devil himself—as the foremost culprit in an attempt to steal your peace. Stealing peace is one of the foremost things the devil tries to steal from every believer in Christ Jesus. (John 10:10 gives us these words of Jesus: "The thief [the devil] does not come except to steal, and to kill, and to destroy. I have come that they may have life, and that they may have it more abundantly.")

_____

_____

_____

_____

_____

_____

## REFLECTION AND RESPONSE

God tells us that the fruit of the Spirit is marked by the quality of peace. Reflect upon the passage below. The fruit of the Spirit should be taken as a whole—they are not "fruits" but *fruit*. The fruit is intended to abide in us.

Note especially the phrase "If we live in the Spirit, let us also walk in the Spirit." We "live" in the Spirit because we received Jesus as our Savior and at the time of our conversion to Christ, we were given God's Spirit resident in us. The fruit of the Spirit came into us at the time we were saved. God's plan is now that we *walk* in the Spirit—manifesting this fruit in our daily lives.

GALATIANS 5:22–25~The fruit of the Spirit is love, joy, peace, longsuffering, kindness, goodness, faithfulness, gentleness, self-control. Against such there is no law. And those who are Christ's have crucified the flesh with its passions and desires. If we live in the Spirit, let us also walk in the Spirit.

*General response:*

_____

_____

_____

_____

*Personal response:*

_____

_____

_____

_____

One of the foremost passages in the New Testament related to our "abiding in peace" is John 15:1–8. Given the fact that peace is part of the fruit that God seeks to manifest in us, I suggest you think *peace* every time you read the word *fruit* in this passage. Reflect upon and respond to various other words and phrases as the Holy Spirit calls your attention to them.

JOHN 15:1–8~[Jesus said:] "I am the true vine, and My Father is the vinedresser. Every branch in Me that does not bear fruit He takes away; and every branch that bears fruit He prunes, that it may bear more fruit. You are already clean because of the word which I have spoken to you. Abide in Me, and I in you. As the branch cannot bear fruit of itself, unless it abides in the vine, neither can you, unless you abide in Me.

"I am the vine, you are the branches. He who abides in Me, and I in him, bears much fruit; for without Me you can do nothing. If anyone does not abide in Me, he is cast out as a branch and is withered; and they gather them and throw them into the fire, and they are burned. If you abide in Me, and My words abide in you, you will ask what you desire, and it shall be done for you. By this My Father is glorified, that you bear much fruit; so you will be My disciples."

*General response:*

_____

_____

_____

_____

*Personal response:*

_____

_____

_____

_____

What other words are related to "abiding"? Make a list of a few of those words below.

_____

_____

_____

_____

Now go back through those words and put an *X* by the words that you believe are true about your own "state of peace."

If you aren't experiencing abiding peace—or if you have a desire to experience more peace in your life, I recommend that you write a letter to God.

## A Letter to God

Express to the Lord fully the frustrations and lack of peace you feel. Pour out your heart to Him about the peace you desire to have. What "abiding" anxieties, fears, worries, frustrations, disappointments, patterns of failure, or resentments do you desire to trade in on *abiding* peace? Ask for God to impart to you an abiding peace that includes joy and a feeling of purpose in every area of your life.

❧

_____

_____

_____

_____

_____

_____

_____

_____

_____

_____

_____

_____

_____

_____

_____

_____

_____

_____

_____

_____

_____

_____

_____

_____

_____

_____

_____

_____

_____

_____

_____

_____

_____

_____

_____

∞

# FOUR

# WHY WE LOSE OUR PEACE

## A NECESSARY FOUNDATION OF FAITH

There is only one way to experience an abiding peace that transcends circumstances. The answer is "by faith." By faith we ask and then trust God to be present in our lives. It is as though we have put a sum of money in the bank, and by faith we write checks because we know that there are funds already deposited to cover our withdrawals. We have asked God to accept and forgive us and to be present in our lives with His abiding peace, and then we go out and live, expecting Him to do the very thing we trust Him to do.

So the foundation for living in God's peace is faith—an active, confident trust in His presence and power to sustain and comfort you no matter what the circumstances you face. (From *Finding Peace*, page 29)

### REFLECTION AND RESPONSE

In virtually all cases, we lay down our peace because we have a "faith failure." We temporarily—or perhaps not so temporarily—lose sight of the greatness and goodness of God. We fail to trust God to love us and to meet our needs. Faith is vitally important to our walk with the Lord. Without faith, we struggle at every turn and can easily be capsized by every storm of life that strikes us.

∞

*Reflect upon and then respond to the following verses in both general and personal ways. Indicate what you believe to be the general message of these passages, and then identify what you believe the Lord has as a personal message to you.*

ROMANS 10:15, 17~It is written:

> "How beautiful are the feet of those who preach the gospel of peace,
> Who bring glad tidings of good things!" . . .
>
> So then faith comes by hearing, and hearing by the word of God.

*General response:*

_____

_____

_____

_____

*Personal response:*

_____

_____

_____

_____

MATTHEW 17:20–21~[Jesus said:] "If you have faith as a mustard seed, you will say to this mountain, 'Move from here to there,' and it will move; and nothing will be impossible for you. However, this kind does not go out except by prayer and fasting."

*General response:*

_____

_____

_____

_____

*Personal response:*

_____

_____

_____

_____

_____

_____

LUKE 17:5~The apostles said to the Lord, "Increase our faith."

*General response:*

_____

_____

_____

_____

_____

*Personal response:*

_____

_____

_____

_____

_____

Are you perhaps feeling at this point that you may be a little "low" on faith? Do you feel that you need to say to the Lord as the disciples did, "Increase my faith"? This is your opportunity to write a letter to God.

## A Letter to God

Express to the Lord your need for increased faith—acknowledge the lack of faith you may feel about a particular situation, circumstance, or relationship. Express any lack of faith you may feel regarding a particular outcome that you truly believe to be God's will for you and others. Ask the Lord to increase your faith.

_____

_____
_____
_____
_____
_____
_____
_____
_____

_____
_____
_____
_____
_____
_____
_____
_____
_____

## An Issue That Can Rob Us of Our Peace: Fear

Some people are so accustomed to responding to every little dip and rise of life with fear and small doses of panic that they can't even imagine there's another way to respond. They are so upset by change of all types that it never even dawns on them that they can live with greater emotional stability.

Say no to fear. Instead, practice a life of trust. Every day begin with the affirmation, "I trust You, Jesus. I count on Your peace and presence today." (From *Finding Peace*, pages 31–32)

### Reflection and Response

Are you struggling with fear today? Are you afraid of a particular person, outcome, or force?

Reflect upon and respond to the passages below.

PHILIPPIANS 2:9–11~Therefore God also has highly exalted [Jesus] and given Him the name which is above every name, that at the name of Jesus every knee should bow, of those in heaven, and of those on earth, and of those under the earth, and that every tongue should confess that Jesus Christ is Lord, to the glory of God the Father.

*General response:*

_____

_____

_____

_____

*Personal response:*

_____

_____

_____

_____

WHY WE LOSE OUR PEACE 51

ROMANS 8:35–39~Who shall separate us from the love of Christ? Shall tribulation, or distress, or persecution, or famine, or nakedness, or peril, or sword? As it is written:

> "For Your sake we are killed all day long;
> We are accounted as sheep for the slaughter."

Yet in all these things we are more than conquerors through Him who loved us. For I am persuaded that neither death nor life, nor angels nor principalities nor powers, nor things present nor things to come, nor height nor depth, nor any other created thing, shall be able to separate us from the love of God which is in Christ Jesus our Lord.

*General response:*

_____

_____

_____

_____

*Personal response:*

_____

_____

_____

_____

The preceding two passages say to me that God does *not* want us to be overcome by fear. He is present with us at all times to help us rebuke and overcome fear. If you are struggling with a particular fear today, now is the time to:

Name your fear:_____

Now write in the space below, in your own handwriting, "Jesus is greater than _____ _____ (and restate your fear)." Do it with large bold letters!

You may need to get an additional sheet of paper . . . but do this for *every* fear you can name in your life.

_____

_____

_____

_____

_____

_____

_____

_____

_____

_____

_____

_____

## AN ISSUE THAT CAN ROB US OF OUR PEACE: THE ENEMY

We can be attacked by our enemy, the devil, who may use various means to cause us to doubt and lose faith in our God. He often does this by priming the pump of doubt with questions—for example, "If God is with you, then why has this happened?" On occasions like this, you have to stand up to the devil, the one who is the ultimate source of any fear that paralyzes you or any anxiety that lingers and hinders you.

I sometimes speak out loud to the devil, the evil power that seeks to thwart the plan of God in our lives. I tell him forthrightly, "Devil, you will *not* have my peace. I refuse to live in fear and worry. I *will* trust God." (From *Finding Peace*, page 32)

## A Grievance Statement Against the Enemy of Your Soul

This is your opportunity to tell the Lord everything you don't like about the devil and what he has been trying to do to your life—both in the past and presently.

Be specific. Ask the Lord to defeat the enemy of your soul at every turn!

_____

_____

_____

_____

_____

_____

_____

_____

_____

_____

_____

_____

_____

_____

_____

_____

_____

_____

_____

## REFLECTION AND RESPONSE

Many people seem to think that the devil and Jesus are on equal footing. They are not. The devil is a created and finite being of a completely different nature from Jesus, who is the divine Son of God and part of the Trinity—Father, Son, and Holy Spirit. Jesus is God. The devil is a creature made by God. Jesus has all authority over the devil. As you reflect upon and respond to the verses below, keep that central fact in mind.

JOHN 10:10~[Jesus said:] "The thief does not come except to steal, and to kill, and to destroy. I have come that they may have life, and that they may have it more abundantly."

*General response:*

_____

_____

_____

_____

*Personal response:*

_____

_____

_____

_____

NOTE: Is there an area in which the devil is coming against your faith today? Jesus has authority over him!

MARK 1:25–27~Jesus rebuked him [the unclean spirit], saying, "Be quiet, and come out of him!" And when the unclean spirit had convulsed him and cried out with a loud voice, he came out of him. Then they were all amazed, so that they questioned among themselves, saying, "What is this? What new doctrine is this? For with authority He commands even the unclean spirits, and they obey Him."

*General response:*

_____

_____

_____

_____

*Personal response:*

_____

_____

_____

_____

JAMES 4:7~Submit to God. Resist the devil and he will flee from you.

*General response:*

_____

_____

_____

_____

*Personal response:*

_____

_____

_____

_____

## AN ISSUE THAT CAN ROB US OF OUR PEACE: SIN

A person can pray repeatedly for God's peace, and believe in his heart for God's peace. He can remind himself of the promises of God and quote them too. But if that person continues to harbor sin in his life and willfully chooses to continue to rebel against God, he will not experience true peace. Even what seems to be a simple matter, like not forgiving someone who offended you, can create havoc in your spirit. The convicting power of the Holy Spirit will continue to *compel* you to face up to what you know is a sin before God. And until you do so, you will have a restlessness and anxiety deep within. The more a person asks God for peace, the more that inner turmoil is likely to increase.

Peace and rebellion cannot coexist!

The only recourse is to confess the rebellion to God, surrender that area of life to Him, and ask Him for help in turning away from that sin and resisting all temptation to return to it. Then God's peace can flow in your life again. (From *Finding Peace*, page 32)

## REFLECTION AND RESPONSE

In an earlier chapter we addressed the great need for you to turn to Jesus as your Savior. Being saved does not mean, of course, that you are immune from all sin or rebellion. The process of being renewed in your heart and mind is just that—a process. We are wise to go to God from time to time and ask Him to cleanse us and to reveal to us any area of our lives in which we need to make changes. As you reflect upon and respond to the following verses, keep in mind your continual need to have God's help in resisting temptation and turning from sin.

ROMANS 6:20–23~When you were slaves of sin . . . what fruit did you have then in the things of which you are now ashamed? For the end of those things is death. But now having been set free from sin, and having become slaves of God, you have your fruit to holiness, and the end, everlasting life. For the wages of sin is death, but the gift of God is eternal life in Christ Jesus our Lord.

*General response:*

_____

_____

_____

_____

*Personal response:*

_____

_____

_____

_____

ISAIAH 1:18–20~"Come now, and let us reason together,"
>Says the LORD,
>"Though your sins are like scarlet,
>They shall be as white as snow;
>Though they are red like crimson,
>They shall be as wool.
>If you are willing and obedient,
>You shall eat the good of the land;
>But if you refuse and rebel,
>You shall be devoured by the sword";
>For the mouth of the LORD has spoken.

*General response:*

_____

_____

_____

_____

*Personal response:*

_____

_____

_____

_____

PSALM 51:1–4~Have mercy upon me, O God,

> According to Your lovingkindness;
> According to the multitude of Your tender mercies,
> Blot out my transgressions.
> Wash me thoroughly from my iniquity,
> And cleanse me from my sin.
> For I acknowledge my transgressions,
> And my sin is always before me.
> Against You, You only, have I sinned,
> And done this evil in Your sight—
> That You may be found just when You speak,
> And blameless when You judge.

*General response:*

_____

_____

_____

_____

*Personal response:*

_____

_____

_____

_____

## AN ISSUE THAT CAN ROB US OF OUR PEACE: GIVING UP PEACE

On a number of occasions through the years when I have felt troubled, anxious, frustrated, or fearful, I blamed other people for "stealing" my peace. I was wrong. The truth is, nobody else should ever have been blamed for my loss of peace. In each and every case, I was the one who laid it down.

Hear me carefully on this point. Nobody can take your peace from you. If you have lost your peace, you have lost it for one main reason—you have surrendered it.

Time and again I hear people say that they are distressed or troubled in spirit by something that happened or something that was said or done against them. I hear variations of "if only she," "if only he," and "if only circumstances had been different" statements. Again, the truth is that no circumstance, situation, person, or organization can steal your inner peace.

We lose our peace because we lay it down. We give it up. We concede it. We abandon it. (From *Finding Peace*, pages 34–35)

## REFLECTION AND RESPONSE

How easy it is to blame others! How difficult it is to accept responsibility for our own behavior! It has been this way since the first man and woman. Read a story you know well—the temptation in the Garden of Eden. Notice the devil's temptation, Eve's response, and Adam's response. Oh, the blame games we have been playing ever since!

GENESIS 3:1–13~Now the serpent was more cunning than any beast of the field which the LORD God had made. And he said to the woman, "Has God indeed said, 'You shall not eat of every tree of the garden'?"

And the woman said to the serpent, "We may eat the fruit of the trees of the garden; but of the fruit of the tree which is in the midst of the garden, God has said, 'You shall not eat it, nor shall you touch it, lest you die.'"

Then the serpent said to the woman, "You will not surely die. For God knows that in the day you eat of it your eyes will be opened, and you will be like God, knowing good and evil."

So when the woman saw that the tree was good for food, that it was pleasant to the eyes, and a tree desirable to make one wise, she took of its fruit and ate. She also gave to her husband with her, and he ate. Then the eyes of both of them were opened, and they knew that they were naked; and they sewed fig leaves together and made themselves coverings.

And they heard the sound of the LORD God walking in the garden in the cool of the day, and Adam and his wife hid themselves from the presence of the LORD God among the trees of the garden.

Then the LORD God called to Adam and said to him, "Where are you?"

So he said, "I heard Your voice in the garden, and I was afraid because I was naked; and I hid myself."

And He said, "Who told you that you were naked? Have you eaten from the tree of which I commanded you that you should not eat?"

Then the man said, "The woman whom You gave to be with me, she gave me of the tree, and I ate."

And the LORD God said to the woman, "What is this you have done?"

The woman said, "The serpent deceived me, and I ate."

*General response:*

_____

_____

_____

_____

_____

*Personal response:*

_____

_____

_____

_____

_____

## DISCUSSION POINT

Neither Adam nor Eve accepted responsibility for their decisions and actions. It is not until you accept personal responsibility for your behavior that you will own up to your own sin—and until you own up to your own sin, there is no genuine confession of sin or request for forgiveness. What difference do you think it may have made if Adam or Eve had taken responsibility for their actions and requested mercy and forgiveness from their Creator?

How important is it today that you face up to your own responsibility in "laying down your peace"?

_____

_____

_____

_____

## AN ISSUE THAT CAN ROB US OF OUR PEACE: LOSING FOCUS

Coping with the news of some kind of tragedy seems to have become part of our daily agenda. A deep sense of foreboding and fearful anticipation seems to hang over our nation. It isn't always major events, however.

We may hear bad news from a physician about our health or the health of a loved one. We may hear bad news about a couple that has separated or divorced, about a child who has run away, about a job that has been lost, or a financial enterprise that has filed bankruptcy. When we see and hear of such terrible news, it is so easy for us to become focused on the negative, to become paralyzed by fear, and sometimes to project that some of these negative possibilities could happen to us so we, too, may become victims. (From *Finding Peace*, page 36)

### REFLECTION AND RESPONSE
Respond to each of the statements below. Be brutally honest with yourself as you do!

|  | ALL THE TIME | SOMETIMES | HARDLY EVER |
|---|---|---|---|
| 1. I routinely and regularly give thanks and praise to God. | _____ | _____ | _____ |
| 2. I believe and am keenly aware that God is *limitless*—He dwells in eternity and operates in infinity. He has *all* things within His understanding and all things under His control. | _____ | _____ | _____ |

ALL THE TIME    SOMETIMES    HARDLY EVER

3. I watch or listen to a great deal of     _____  _____  _____
   news and since most of the news is
   negative, I tend to dwell upon and
   talk about negative situations.

4. I find it difficult to get rid of negative    _____  _____  _____
   emotions—it seems easy for me to
   slide into anxiety, panic, fear, or worry.

5. I weigh every situation I face or hear    _____  _____  _____
   about against the teachings and
   example of Jesus.

Go back and review your responses. Are they responses you truly believe God desires for you to have? Are they responses conducive to finding and abiding in a state of peace?

_____

_____

_____

What do you need to do to make changes in your pattern of thinking? How might you regain your focus? Are there specific things you can do, starting *today*, to turn your own thinking and feeling away from a negative, limited, fear-prone, and world-oriented perspective and toward a positive, limitless, faith-filled, and godly perspective? Be specific in citing things you can do.

_____

_____

_____

_____

Go back and underline, circle, or highlight those things you are actually willing to make a commitment before God to *do*, starting today.

## THANKS AND PRAISE

Now is the time to offer to the Lord your thanks and praise that He is the One who has given each of us a measure of faith to use. He is the One who increases our faith. He is the One who enables us to overcome all obstacles to our faith, even fear and sin. He is the One who enables us to withstand the accusations, temptations, or assaults of the devil. He is the One who calls us to *keep* our peace, rather than lay it down, and to *maintain* our focus on what God desires for us, rather than lose our focus and begin to drift into a worldly downward spiral into negative thoughts and feelings.

List at least ten things for which you are thankful to God! Be specific. (For example: Thank You, Lord, for keeping me from giving in to the temptation I faced last Tuesday afternoon. I praise You, Lord, for taking all fear out of my heart as I began to tell my neighbor about Jesus.)

_____

_____

_____

_____

_____

_____

_____

_____

_____

_____

_____

_____

_____

_____

∞

# FIVE ESSENTIAL BELIEFS FOR A PEACEFUL HEART

## NO LOSS OF POWER OR MIGHT

God has never been out of control over His creation for one fraction of a second since the beginning of time. He hasn't lost one measure of His power or might. He is just as omnipotent, omniscient, omnipresent, and all-loving.

Understanding the ways of God always leads to an understanding that God will act in a way that brings about eternal blessings for His children. It is what we *believe* that makes it possible to ask the right questions in the face of tragedy. (From *Finding Peace*, pages 42–43)

## *A Letter to God*

When tragedies or calamities strike, many people begin to ask: Was God in control? Could God have prevented what happened? Did God *allow* what happened? Did He have a purpose for allowing this to happen?

The answer to each of these questions is a resounding "yes."

People also tend to ask, Why did this happen? That question often has no answer—at least not one that a person can discern clearly in the moment or immediate future. If a person continues to ask why, he likely will get bogged down in his spirit and is likely to become discouraged, depressed, and angry with God.

The far more important questions to ask are these: God, what do You want me to learn in response to this? What now? How shall I respond?

These questions can move a person forward with direction, purpose, new energy, and genuine peace.

Have you struggled to understand the reason for a tragedy in your life? Are you struggling today with "why" questions and questions about the omnipotence, omniscience, omnipresence, or love of God?

Take this opportunity to write a letter to God about your feelings. I encourage you to address the *What do You want me to learn? What now?* and *How shall I respond?* questions in your letter.

_____

_____

_____

_____

_____

_____

_____

_____

_____

_____

_____

_____

_____

_____

_____

_____

_____

_____

_____

## REFLECTION AND RESPONSE

A passage of the Bible that deals with questions we tend to ask God in times of tragedy or crisis is found in 2 Chronicles 20. King Jehoshaphat was in an extremely difficult situation. Three great armies came against Jerusalem simultaneously— Moabite soldiers, Ammonite soldiers, and soldiers of the people of Mount Seir. Jehoshaphat was afraid. The Bible tells us he "set himself to seek the LORD, and [he] proclaimed a fast throughout all Judah." He called for the elders of the people throughout the land to come to Jerusalem to help him seek help from the Lord. As you read through the verses below, note especially the questions Jehoshaphat asked of the Lord—and then the Lord's response. Highlight or mark key words and phrases that stand out to you in a special way.

❧

*Reflect upon and then respond to the verses below in both* general *and* personal *ways. Indicate what you believe to be the general message of these passages, and then identify what you believe the Lord has as a personal message to you.*

2 CHRONICLES 20:5–12~Then Jehoshaphat stood in the assembly of Judah and Jerusalem, in the house of the LORD, before the new court, and said: "O LORD God of our fathers, are You not God in heaven, and do You not rule over all the kingdoms of the nations, and in Your hand is there not power and might, so that no one is able to withstand You? Are You not our God, who drove out the inhabitants of this land before Your people Israel, and gave it to the descendants of Abraham Your friend forever? And they dwell in it, and have built You a sanctuary in it for Your name, saying, 'If disaster comes upon us—sword, judgment, pestilence, or famine—we will stand before this temple and in Your presence (for Your name is in this temple), and cry out to You in our affliction, and You will hear and save.' And now, here are the people of Ammon, Moab, and Mount Seir—whom You would not let Israel invade when they came out of the land of Egypt, but they turned from them and did not destroy them—here they are, rewarding us by coming to throw us out of Your possession which You have given us to inherit. O our God, will You not judge them? For we have no power against this great multitude that is coming against us; nor do we know what to do, but our eyes are upon You."

*General response:*

_____

_____

_____

_____

*Personal response:*

_____

_____

_____

_____

Have you been in an experience similar to this one? A situation in which people were coming against you even though you were doing what was right? How did you respond? Did you reach the position in which you had to admit, "I have no power in this and I don't know what to do, but my eyes are on You, Lord"?

What happened? Who was involved?

_____

_____

_____

_____

How did God respond to you?

_____

_____

_____

How important were your *beliefs* in your time of tragedy? How did your faith sustain you?

_____

_____

_____

_____

## AN ESSENTIAL BELIEF FOR PEACE:
## GOD IS ABSOLUTELY SOVEREIGN

Recognizing and accepting the truth that God is sovereign over absolutely everything is vital for your inner peace. God is absolutely sovereign—which means that nothing related to you is beyond His watchful eye and loving care. (From *Finding Peace*, page 43)

### REFLECTION AND RESPONSE

Psalm 91 is a wonderful psalm that addresses the sovereignty of God. Read through this psalm slowly and note key words or phrases that stand out to you in a special way. What does this passage reveal to you about the nature of God?

PSALM 91~He who dwells in the secret place of the Most High
    Shall abide under the shadow of the Almighty.
    I will say of the LORD, "He is my refuge and my fortress;
    My God, in Him I will trust."
    Surely He shall deliver you from the snare of the fowler
    And from the perilous pestilence.
    He shall cover you with His feathers,
    And under His wings you shall take refuge;
    His truth shall be your shield and buckler.
    You shall not be afraid of the terror by night,
    Nor of the arrow that flies by day,
    Nor of the pestilence that walks in darkness,
    Nor of the destruction that lays waste at noonday.

A thousand may fall at your side,

And ten thousand at your right hand;

But it shall not come near you.

Only with your eyes shall you look,

And see the reward of the wicked.

Because you have made the LORD, who is my refuge,

Even the Most High, your dwelling place,

No evil shall befall you,

Nor shall any plague come near your dwelling;

For He shall give His angels charge over you,

To keep you in all your ways.

In their hands they shall bear you up,

Lest you dash your foot against a stone.

You shall tread upon the lion and the cobra,

The young lion and the serpent you shall trample underfoot.

"Because he has set his love upon Me, therefore I will deliver him;

I will set him on high, because he has known My name.

He shall call upon Me, and I will answer him;

I will be with him in trouble;

I will deliver him and honor him.

With long life I will satisfy him,

And show him My salvation."

*General response:*

_____

_____

_____

_____

*Personal response:*

_____

_____

_____

_____

Can you recall an experience in which God protected you in a unique way? How did God use that experience to teach you more about His sovereignty and His love?

_____

_____

_____

_____

## AN ESSENTIAL BELIEF FOR PEACE: GOD IS YOUR PROVIDER

It is not part of God's plan for you to lie awake at night, tossing and turning and wondering, *How am I going to pay my bills if I lose my job? What am I going to do when I retire if the stock market continues to decline? How am I going to provide for my family if my company goes through bankruptcy?* or any other concern that you may have.

The need you have may not be a need for food, water, or clothing. It may be a need for emotional healing, spiritual deliverance, a new opportunity for employment, reconciliation of a broken relationship, or any one of a host of other internal or relational needs. Friend, God is able to meet that need! He is the God who provides for His people all things that are required for a full, satisfying, and purposeful life. (From *Finding Peace*, page 48)

### REFLECTION AND RESPONSE

As you read through the passages below, reflect especially upon the different ways in which God has provided for His people. What He has done for others, He will do for you!

Each of these examples is about a practical and material need—the needs you have today for food, shelter, clothing, education, transportation, and so forth are also practical and material in nature. Look for the deeper truth in each of these stories about God being your Provider for all you need.

EXODUS 16:35~The children of Israel ate manna forty years, until they came to an inhabited land; they ate manna until they came to the border of the land of Canaan.

*General response:*

_____

_____

_____

_____

*Personal response:*

_____

_____

_____

_____

### DISCUSSION POINT

The very specific rules for gathering, using, and storing manna are given earlier in Exodus 16. I encourage you to read this entire chapter and note some of these specifics. How much trust was required on the part of the Israelites that sufficient manna would appear day by day?

What importance does God place upon having a Sabbath Day—a day without the "gathering" of material substance?

_____

_____

_____

_____

EXODUS 17:1–7~Then all the congregation of the children of Israel set out on their journey from the Wilderness of Sin, according to the commandment of the LORD, and camped in Rephidim; but there was no water for the people to drink. Therefore the people contended with Moses, and said, "Give us water, that we may drink."

So Moses said to them, "Why do you contend with me? Why do you tempt the LORD?"

And the people thirsted there for water, and the people complained against Moses, and said, "Why is it you have brought us up out of Egypt, to kill us and our children and our livestock with thirst?"

So Moses cried out to the LORD, saying, "What shall I do with this people? They are almost ready to stone me!"

And the LORD said to Moses, "Go on before the people, and take with you some of the elders of Israel. Also take in your hand your rod with which you struck the river, and go. Behold, I will stand before you there on the rock in Horeb; and you shall strike the rock, and water will come out of it, that the people may drink."

And Moses did so in the sight of the elders of Israel. So he called the name of the place Massah and Meribah, because of the contention of the children of Israel, and because they tempted the LORD, saying, "Is the LORD among us or not?"

*General response:*

_____

_____

_____

_____

_____

*Personal response:*

_____

_____

_____

_____

_____

## WHO IS IN CONTROL OF YOUR MATERIAL RESOURCES?

Ask yourself, "Who is in control of my material resources?" If you think you are in control, you're wrong. You certainly have a responsibility to be a good steward, or manager, of the resources God has given to you, but you aren't in control of your income or the material substance that comes your way. Everything you have today is a gift from God to you. He is the One who has given you the energy, vitality, health, ideas, and opportunities that have led to your "possessing" all that you have. Surely as He has provided for you all your life, He will continue to provide for you as you trust Him, obey Him, and seek to do His will. (From *Finding Peace*, page 51)

∞

### THANKS AND PRAISE

Think back over all the many ways in which God has provided *all* that you need— the air you breathe, the water you drink, the job you have, your family and friends. Make a list of at least ten things you recognize as God providing for you!

_____

_____

_____

_____

_____

_____

_____

_____

_____

## AN ESSENTIAL BELIEF FOR PEACE: GOD MADE YOU THE WAY YOU ARE FOR A PURPOSE

Your race, culture, language, nationality, sex, and many attributes of your physical being are God's choices. God also gave you certain talents and aptitudes that make it easier for you to acquire and perfect certain skills. He gave you a degree of intelligence to develop through study and to apply to practical matters. He gave you a basic personality—even from birth some babies seem more outgoing and others seem more passive. At the time you accepted Jesus Christ as your Savior, God gave you certain spiritual gifts to use in ministry to others. The way in which you express those gifts is uniquely linked to the talents He has given you and the skills He has helped you develop.

All these traits and factors taken as a whole make you a unique person on this earth. Nobody who has ever lived before you has been just like you. Nobody alive on the earth today is just like you, not even a sibling who may be your twin. Nobody who will ever live will be just like you, including your children. You are a unique and very special creation of God, designed for a particular purpose on this earth that God has had in mind from eternity past. Accept who God made you to be! (From *Finding Peace*, pages 53–54)

∾

## Thanks and Praise

Take a few minutes to reflect on your unique qualities, traits, gifts, and spiritual gifts. Make a list of at least ten of these unique qualities God has given you and thank God for them! He is your Creator, your Designer, your Maker!

_____

_____

_____

_____

_____

_____

_____

_____

_____

_____

## REFLECTION AND RESPONSE

Reflect on the ways in which you are developing the potential God has given you.

- Are you changing what you can change in order to be the best at whatever you undertake? ("Best" is related to your own potential, not comparison to others.) What more might you do to pursue your *best*?

_____

_____

_____

_____

- Are there lies you have been told all your life that you need to *reject* because they simply aren't what *God* says about you? If so, identify them!

_____

_____

_____

_____

- What is God's *truth* that replaces each of these lies?

_____

_____

_____

_____

# AN ESSENTIAL BELIEF FOR PEACE: GOD HAS A PLACE WHERE YOU TRULY BELONG

God tells us plainly that we are to have fellowship with other believers in the church. The Bible clearly tells us that we are not to forsake the assembling of ourselves together (Heb.

10:25). Why? Because every person in the body of Christ has been given a unique personality, set of abilities and skills, at least one ministry gift, and natural talents. God expects each of us to share these unique attributes with other believers in a loving, generous way so needs within any particular body of believers will be met and the gospel will be extended to those outside the church. We need one another in the church. We are part of one another. (From *Finding Peace*, page 61)

## REFLECTION AND RESPONSE

In the passage below, the apostle Paul identified for the believers in Rome eight "ministry gifts." As you read through this passage, note especially the gift that you believe God has given to you.

ROMANS 12:4–8~For as we have many members in one body, but all the members do not have the same function, so we, being many, are one body in Christ, and individually members of one another. Having then gifts differing according to the grace that is given to us, let us use them: if prophecy, let us prophesy in proportion to our faith; or ministry, let us use it in our ministering; he who teaches, in teaching; he who exhorts, in exhortation; he who gives, with liberality; he who leads, with diligence; he who shows mercy, with cheerfulness.

*General response:*

_____

_____

_____

_____

*Personal response:*

_____

_____

_____

_____

In the passage below, the apostle Paul identified the "spirit" in which ministry gifts are to be used in the church. Identify key words and phrases that stand out to you.

ROMANS 12:9–21 ~ Let love be without hypocrisy. Abhor what is evil. Cling to what is good. Be kindly affectionate to one another with brotherly love, in honor giving preference to one another; not lagging in diligence, fervent in spirit, serving the Lord; rejoicing in hope, patient in tribulation, continuing steadfastly in prayer; distributing to the needs of the saints, given to hospitality.

Bless those who persecute you; bless and do not curse. Rejoice with those who rejoice, and weep with those who weep. Be of the same mind toward one another. Do not set your mind on high things, but associate with the humble. Do not be wise in your own opinion.

Repay no one evil for evil. Have regard for good things in the sight of all men. If it is possible, as much as depends on you, live peaceably with all men. Beloved, do not avenge yourselves, but rather give place to wrath; for it is written, "Vengeance is Mine, I will repay," says the Lord. Therefore

> "If your enemy is hungry, feed him;
> If he is thirsty, give him a drink;
> For in so doing you will heap coals of fire on his head."

Do not be overcome by evil, but overcome evil with good.

_General response:_

_____

_____

_____

_____

*Personal response:*

_____

_____

_____

_____

∾

## DISCUSSION POINT

In what ways do you need others who are in your church? In what ways do others in your church need you?

In what ways do the ministry gifts in Romans 12:4–8 manifest themselves in your church?

_____

_____

_____

_____

_____

_____

# AN ESSENTIAL BELIEF FOR PEACE:
# GOD HAS A PLAN FOR YOUR FULFILLMENT

For real inner peace, a person needs to know that he or she is competent, able, capable, and skilled at doing something. The "something" may be a task that the world as a whole considers to be a menial chore or service. Nonetheless, if you can do that task, and you know that you do it well, you are competent! There's a wonderful sense of peace that comes when you know you are capable of putting in a good performance or doing a good job.

God will not lead you to "become" something without aiding you to become the best you can possibly be in that area. He will not give you a talent and then fail to give you opportunities for discovering, using, developing, practicing, and perfecting it. (From *Finding Peace*, pages 64–66)

## REFLECTION AND RESPONSE

Can you identify quickly several things that you know, without doubt, that you are good at doing? List them!

_____

_____

_____

_____

Stop to reflect for a moment on the fact that you may be good at those things today, but five to ten years ago you may not have been good at these things.

Generally speaking, most people feel a certain degree of incompetence about certain things in life. Can you identify several things about which you have self-doubts? Perhaps it is something in your work that you know you don't really know well, or a skill related to being a good spouse or parent that is giving you some concern. List several self-doubts below:

_____

_____

_____

_____

Take another look at this list you have made. Ask yourself, "If I get good instruction, can I become competent in this? If I practice more at this, can I become competent?" Put an X by every item to which you could respond with a "yes" answer.

Now, ask yourself, "Where and when can I get the instruction I need? How can I work into my daily or weekly schedule more practice in this life skill?" Write out a simple strategy for what you can do to become more competent:

_____

_____

_____

_____

# INCOMPETENCE VS INADEQUACY

There's nothing wrong with feeling a certain amount of incompetence or inadequacy. Incompetence and inadequacy are two different things: Incompetence says, "I can't do this because I'm lacking something." Inadequacy says, "I can't do this in my own strength."

The very fact that you are capable of continuing to learn and develop tells you that you will never be fully competent at anything. Each of us will always have plenty of room for growth, and that's part of God's design for us. We also will never be fully adequate because we will always have a need for God to do in us, for us, and through us what He alone can do. God is the author and finisher of our lives; not only of our faith, but of all aspects of the potential He has built into us.

Anytime you feel inadequate, go to God and say, "I feel inadequate. I'm trusting You to be my adequacy."

If you feel ignorant, trust God to be your source of wisdom.

If you feel weak or exhausted, trust God to be your strength.

If you feel yourself totally without adequate resources, trust God to provide what you need. (From *Finding Peace*, pages 66–68)

## REFLECTION AND RESPONSE

One of the most competent men in the New Testament was the apostle Paul. He was an excellent communicator, a skilled traveler, a highly proficient teacher, a man well-versed in the Scriptures, and a man highly sensitive to the leading of the Holy Spirit. Even so, he knew that he did not succeed in his own strength. He was totally reliant upon the Lord. As you reflect upon the verses below, note any words or phrases that stand out in a special way to you.

2 CORINTHIANS 3:5~Not that we are sufficient of ourselves to think of anything as being from ourselves, but our sufficiency is from God.

*General response:*

_____

_____

_____

_____

*Personal response:*

_____

_____

_____

_____

PHILIPPIANS 4:13~I can do all things through Christ who strengthens me.

*General response:*

_____

_____

_____

_____

*Personal response:*

_____

_____

_____

_____

### DISCUSSION POINT

What does it mean to be sufficient or to trust the Lord for sufficiency? As an individual? As a group of people who are following the Lord?

_____

_____

_____

_____

_____

_____

How does Christ strengthen you?

_____

_____

_____

Moses was a man who struggled with self-doubts about his competency, not when he was a teenager or young man, but when he was eighty years old! He had been working as a shepherd for his father-in-law, the priest of Midian, for nearly forty years after he fled Pharaoh's court in the wake of murdering an Egyptian. (See Exodus 2:11–3:1.) While out with the flock on the "back of the desert," Moses came to Mount Horeb and there, the Angel of the Lord appeared to him in a flame of fire from the midst of a bush. The bush burned with fire, but was not consumed. Moses turned aside to see this unusual sight and God spoke to him from the burning bush. He revealed to Moses that He was the God of Abraham, the God of Isaac, and the God of Jacob and told Moses he was standing on holy ground.

As you read through the dialogue between God and Moses below, note certain words and phrases that seem to stand out to you in a special way. Especially note the questions Moses asked God. Ask the Holy Spirit to reveal to you what He desires for you to learn.

EXODUS 3:7–14; 4:1–5, 10–15~The LORD said: "I have surely seen the oppression of My people who are in Egypt, and have heard their cry because of their task-masters, for I know their sorrows. So I have come down to deliver them out of the hand of the Egyptians, and to bring them up from that land to a good and large land, to a land flowing with milk and honey, to the place of the Canaanites and the Hittites and the Amorites and the Perezzites and the Hivites and the Jebusites. Now there-fore, behold, the cry of the children of Israel has come to Me, and I have also seen the oppression with which the Egyptians oppress them. Come now, therefore, and

I will send you to Pharaoh that you may bring My people, the children of Israel, out of Egypt."

But Moses said to God, "Who am I that I should go to Pharaoh, and that I should bring the children of Israel out of Egypt?"

So He said, "I will certainly be with you. And this shall be a sign to you that I have sent you: When you have brought the people out of Egypt, you shall serve God on this mountain."

Then Moses said to God, "Indeed, when I come to the children of Israel and say to them, 'The God of your fathers has sent me to you,' and they say to me, 'What is His name?' what shall I say to them?"

And God said to Moses, "I AM WHO I AM." And He said, "Thus you shall say to the children of Israel, 'I AM has sent me to you.'"

Then Moses answered and said, "But suppose they will not believe me or listen to my voice; suppose they say, 'The LORD has not appeared to you.'" . . .

So the LORD said to him, "What is that in your hand?"

He said, "A rod."

And He said, "Cast it on the ground." So he cast it on the ground, and it became a serpent; and Moses fled from it. Then the LORD said to Moses, "Reach out your hand and take it by the tail (and he reached out his hand and caught it, and it became a rod in his hand), that they may believe that the LORD God of their fathers, the God of Abraham, the God of Isaac, and the God of Jacob, has appeared to you." . . .

Then Moses said to the LORD, "O my Lord, I am not eloquent, neither before nor since You have spoken to Your servant; but I am slow of speech and slow of tongue."

So the LORD said to him, "Who has made man's mouth? Or who makes the mute, the deaf, the seeing, or the blind? Have not I, the LORD? Now therefore, go, and I will be with your mouth and teach you what you shall say."

But he said, "O my Lord, please send by the hand of whomever else You may send."

So the anger of the LORD was kindled against Moses, and He said: "Is not Aaron the Levite your brother? I know that he can speak well. And look, he is also coming out to meet you. When he sees you, he will be glad in his heart. Now you shall speak to him, and put the words in his mouth. And I will be with your mouth and with his mouth, and I will teach you what you shall do."

*General response:*

_____

_____

_____

_____

*Personal response:*

_____

_____

_____

_____

NOTE: How would you answer the Lord if He asked you, "What is in your hand?"
What abilities, skills, or possessions do you have that God might use to further the gospel of Jesus Christ on this earth?

∞

## DISCUSSION POINT

To what degree do you believe the Lord was attempting to move Moses from a position of feeling "incompetent" to a position of "inadequacy"—from a position of feeling that he was lacking in ability, to a position in which he needed to rely totally on
the Lord for his strength? How important is it for a person, or a church group as a
whole, to come before the Lord with a sense of inadequacy, a sense of "needing"
God's presence and strength?

_____

_____

_____

_____

_____

_____

# NEVER DISCOUNT GOD'S PURPOSE FOR YOUR LIFE

When God reveals His purpose to you, never discount that purpose. Never say to others, "I'm just a . . ."

Every form of honest, morally sound, godly work is worthy of reward, worthy of your doing it to the best of your ability, and worthy of respect. (From *Finding Peace*, page 70)

## REFLECTION AND RESPONSE

Can you state in a clear, direct way what you believe to be your foremost purpose in life? You might consider this a "mission statement" for your life—a statement about what it is you believe God has called you to do, to be, to produce, or to be a "spokesperson" for. Write out your purpose below:

_____

_____

_____

_____

_____

_____

_____

_____

_____

_____

_____

_____

_____

_____

_____

_____

## A Grievance Statement

I have placed great emphasis on these basic beliefs in *Finding Peace*:

- God is absolutely sovereign and in full control of all things at all times.

- God is your provider—materially, physically, emotionally, and spiritually.

- God considers you to be worthy and lovable—He has made you the way you are for His purposes.

- God cares about your loneliness and wants you to experience fellowship with others.

- God has a plan and purpose for your life that will be fulfilling for you.

If you do not believe these basic truths about God and the relationship He desires to have with you, you cannot experience a genuine, lasting peace.

What God says to us about ourselves—our value as a friend, our abilities and talents, our purpose—is often very different from what people have said to us. So many times I encounter people who have been told as a child by a parent, teacher, or some other authority figure, that they will never amount to anything, are unlovable, unworthy, or incompetent. These people carry around a load of negative emotional baggage that keeps them from being truly at peace in their innermost being. Is that true for you? If so, this is your opportunity to write a grievance statement.

Identify the person who put you down or held you back. Identify the person who failed to prepare you with a positive self-image or a positive reliance upon the Lord for your adequacy and sufficiency. Identify the enemy of your soul who did his utmost to keep you from fully embracing all of your talents, pursuing and developing your abilities, and engaging in the ministry God has for you.

Be specific, concrete, and complete. Don't hold anything back. Write out your grievance in the space provided or on another sheet of paper.

_____

_____

_____

_____

_____

_____

_____

_____

_____

_____

_____

_____

_____

_____

As you bring your grievance statement before the Lord, voice to Him your reliance upon Him to help you fully believe that He is in control, that He loves you, that He has a plan and purpose for you, that He is providing all you need, and that He is seeking your best at all times.

∞

# SIX

# HOW YOUR THOUGHT LIFE
# AFFECTS YOUR PEACE

## YOUR THOUGHTS CONTROL YOUR WORDS AND DEEDS

What you think makes a huge difference in what you say and do. Your thoughts, which flow out of your basic beliefs, are like the traffic controllers of your life. They determine where you go, what activities you pursue, how you pursue them, the people you are willing to include in your life, and many other factors, all of which result in your ultimate success or failure.

The way you think about other people also becomes the way you treat other people. The way you think about situations becomes the way you respond to them. Those things you think are important become your "priorities," and in turn, your priorities determine how you plan a week, schedule a day, or map out a set of plans and goals. (From *Finding Peace*, page 73)

### REFLECTION AND RESPONSE

The Bible has a great deal to say about the importance of a person's thoughts. The concept of "renewal of the mind" is vitally important to your growth and maturity in Christ Jesus—to "renew the mind" is basically to "change the way you think" so that your thoughts line up with God's thoughts.

As you read through the verses below, note specific words or phrases that seem to stand out to you in a special way.

*Reflect upon and then respond to the verses below in both general and personal ways. Indicate what you believe to be the general message of these passages, and then identify what you believe the Lord has as a personal message to you.*

ROMANS 12:2~Do not be conformed to this world, but be transformed by the renewing of your mind, that you may prove what is that good and acceptable and perfect will of God.

*General response:*

_____

_____

_____

_____

*Personal response:*

_____

_____

_____

_____

PROVERBS 12:5, 8~The thoughts of the righteous are right,
        But the counsels of the wicked are deceitful . . .
        A man will be commended according to his wisdom,
        But he who is of a perverse heart will be despised.

*General response:*

_____

_____

_____

_____

*Personal response:*

_____

_____

_____

_____

PROVERBS 23:7~As he thinks in his heart, so is he.

*General response:*

_____

_____

_____

_____

*Personal response:*

_____

_____

_____

_____

## OUR NEED TO CHANGE THE WAY WE THINK

Most people aren't really what they think they are. Most people have an overly inflated, in-accurate, or overly negative impression of themselves. Our human tendency is toward pride, error, low self-esteem, or a combination of these. Our self-perceptions are often very skewed by self-justification, selfish desires, or the influence of others around us.

Many people have a thought life that is a little like concrete—it's all mixed up and extremely rigid! They have acquired a mishmash of both good and bad thinking. They have confused that with their fleshly desires and have hardened their hearts to any godly change.

God's Word refers to such people as "stiff-necked" or as having a "heart of stone." They are stubbornly intent on living their lives according to their own rules and emotional impulses, with very little regard for the ways in which they hurt others, and virtually no regard for what God desires. (From *Finding Peace*, pages 73–74)

## REFLECTION AND RESPONSE

The plain and simple fact about our thinking is this: It needs to line up with the way God thinks. Our opinions need to be *His* opinions. Our evaluations need to be *His* evaluations. What we think of ourselves and others needs to line up with what *God* thinks of us and others. And yes, God does think about us! He does require a change in our thinking!

As you read and reflect upon the verses below, highlight any words or phrases that seem to stand out to you in a special way. What might God be showing you about your own stiff neck or heart of stone? What might God be trying to reveal to you about the way you think? How willing are you to allow Him to refashion your opinions and evaluations of your own self and of other people?

JEREMIAH 29:11~For I know the thoughts that I think toward you, says the LORD, thoughts of peace and not of evil, to give you a future and a hope.

*General response:*

_____

_____

_____

_____

*Personal response:*

_____

_____

_____

_____

ISAIAH 55:8–9~"For My thoughts are not your thoughts,
            Nor are your ways My ways," says the LORD.
            "For as the heavens are higher than the earth,
            So are My ways higher than your ways,
            And My thoughts than your thoughts."

*General response:*

_____

_____

_____

_____

*Personal response:*

_____

_____

_____

_____

PSALM 139:23–24~Search me, O God, and know my heart;
            Try me, and know my anxieties;
            And see if there is any wicked way in me,
            And lead me in the way everlasting.

*General response:*

_____

_____

_____

_____

*Personal response:*

_____

_____

_____

_____

_____

∞

### DISCUSSION POINT

How difficult is it to change the way you think and, especially, to change your
thoughts so they line up with God's thoughts?

_____

_____

_____

_____

## SEVEN CATEGORIES OF PEACE-DESTROYING THOUGHTS

There are seven categories of thoughts that will do great damage to your peace:

### 1. SINFUL THOUGHTS

These thoughts include lustful desires for power, money, prestige, or sex outside marriage.
Lust and peace cannot inhabit the same heart. Lust is a controlling desire—lust both entices and
compels a person to do what is contrary to God's commandments. Sinful thoughts also include
anger, resentment, envy, bitterness, hatred, hostility, controlling fears, and thoughts of revenge.

### 2. SELF-LIMITING THOUGHTS

The more you put yourself down, the more you deny God's power to raise you up. The
more you diminish the gifts and talents God has built into your life, the less likely you will
be to seek to develop those gifts and talents.

### 3. ERRONEOUS THOUGHTS

Sometimes we think "incorrectly" because we are ignorant. We simply don't know the
motivation of a person, the truth about a circumstance, or the facts of a situation.

## 4. UNREALISTIC THOUGHTS

Anytime people set goals for their lives that require great striving, intense frustration, repeated failures, and manipulation of others—those are unrealistic goals. They are not within the realm of their God-given talents and abilities. It is beyond God's plan and purpose for their lives.

Any idea you pursue that is contrary to God's purpose for your life, His commands in the Bible, or the plan of salvation is an idea that is not rooted in reality. It is an idea that has a built-in flaw. It is an idea that will cause you great inner agitation, not peace.

God will not lead you into unrealistic thinking.

## 5. REBELLIOUS THOUGHTS

Those who engage in rebellious thinking are those who say, "I know what God's Word says, but I'm going to do what I want to do anyway."

## 6. OBSESSIVE THOUGHTS

Obsessive thoughts are thoughts that harass and dominate a person, dividing his mind and fracturing his thinking. The person who has an obsession cannot focus on anything other than his or her attainment of the desired object or goal.

## 7. ENSLAVED THOUGHTS

Enslaved thinking is one step beyond obsessive thinking. A person moves into enslaved thinking when he wants to think about something else and can't. Most addicts are victims of enslaved thinking. They cannot escape thinking about the thing to which they are addicted. The alcoholic is always planning the next drink. The drug user is always thinking about the next fix. Thoughts related to the addiction fill every waking hour. (From *Finding Peace*, pages 75–77, 82, 84, 86, 88)

## A Letter to God

People seem to gravitate in their thinking toward one or more of these peace-destroying thoughts, and this is especially so in people who find that they do not live in an abiding state of God's peace. I encourage you to write a letter to God about your own thought life.

As you read through the list of seven peace-destroying thought patterns, did one of these stand out to you? Did you find yourself saying, "That's my problem"?

Confess that peace-destroying way of thinking to the Lord. Tell Him about your struggle in controlling your thoughts or in changing the way you tend to think. Ask Him to speak to you through His Word so you truly can experience a renewal of your mind.

## ERRORS IN OUR THINKING ABOUT GOD

Many people tend to think the worst about God, rather than to believe the best about Him!

Through the years I have repeatedly heard God blamed for a tragedy, catastrophe, or the death of a beloved family member or friend. God doesn't send tragedies into a person's life. That's the work of the enemy of our souls. The person who blames God for things that have gone wrong in his or her life—including various injustices, abuses, or prejudices held against him or her—is a person who is unwilling to trust God. The truth is that trusting God is at the heart of peace.

*Errors in our thinking about God's Word.* Many people have incorrect concepts about the Bible. They believe it isn't accurate, it isn't the Word of God, it isn't valid for today's world, or that it doesn't relate to their everyday lives. They are wrong on all counts. The person who doesn't trust the accuracy and truthfulness of God's Word is a person who has no foundation for finding, receiving, or accepting God's offer of peace.

*Errors in our thinking about salvation.* Three of the biggest errors that I hear about salvation are these:

- *I've sinned too much to be saved.* The Lord is frequently portrayed in the Scriptures as being "long-suffering" toward us—which means He is patient. He is portrayed as being filled with mercy toward us, which means He stands ready to forgive the moment we turn to Him to confess our sins and receive His mercy. From the foundation of time, His desire is always that we receive Jesus as our Savior and live with Him forever.

- *I've committed the unpardonable sin.* The very fact that you are questioning if you have committed the unpardonable sin means that you haven't. Those who commit the unpardonable sin are those who have rejected God to the point that they have absolutely no desire to know God or have a relationship with Him. They have completely cut themselves off from any awareness of God and they are void of conscience. I seriously doubt that you have done this if you are reading this book!

- *I'm saved right now, but I'm not sure my salvation will last.* The Bible tells us that those who receive Jesus as their Savior are born anew in their spirit. What is "birthed" by the Holy Spirit can never be "un-birthed" by Him. The Holy Spirit "seals" us as God's children forever. There's nothing we or anybody else can do to "unseal" what God has sealed.

You may walk away from God and come to a place where you no longer experience close fellowship with Him. You may reject the convicting nudges of the Holy Spirit in pursuit of your own sinful desires. You may fail to pursue God's call on your life and miss out on many of the eternal rewards God has planned for you. But I believe you cannot "undo" your salvation. (From *Finding Peace*, pages 78–81)

## REFLECTION AND RESPONSE

The Bible has scores of verses that express the truths presented in the statements above. Below, I'm going to provide only a few key verses related to God's nature, God's Word, and God's gift of salvation. As you read through them, note especially words or phrases that seem to stand out to you. Ask yourself as you read, *Do I believe this with all my heart, without doubt?*

JUDE 21~Keep yourselves in the love of God, looking for the mercy of our Lord Jesus Christ unto eternal life.

*General response:*

_____

_____

_____

_____

*Personal response:*

_____

_____

_____

_____

JOHN 3:16~For God so loved the world that He gave His only begotten Son, that whoever believes in Him should not perish but have everlasting life.

*General response:*

_____

_____

_____

_____

*Personal response:*

_____

_____

_____

_____

ROMANS 8:38–39~For I am persuaded that neither death nor life, nor angels nor principalities nor powers, nor things present nor things to come, nor height nor depth, nor any other created thing, shall be able to separate us from the love of God which is in Christ Jesus our Lord.

*General response:*

_____

_____

_____

_____

*Personal response:*

_____

_____

_____

_____

## DISCUSSION POINT

When it comes to experiencing the abiding peace of God, how important has it been, or is it presently, that you have a firm assurance of God's love, a firm belief in the truth of God's Word, and a rock-solid belief that your salvation gives you eternal security with the Lord?

_____

_____

_____

_____

# THREE TYPES OF REBELLIOUS THINKING

*"All-too-natural" rebellion.* There's a form of rebellion that is rooted in this choice: "It seemed natural to me." Anytime you have an idea that just "feels right" in your emotions or "feels like the natural human thing to do," stop yourself. Reevaluate what you are thinking about doing. Weigh it against the commands of God. Most of the impulses of the natural man are rooted in selfish desires—greed, lust, a craving for power or control.

*"Hesitation" rebellion.* A person may know with great clarity and confirmation what God wants her to do, but she waits, saying, "I'm thinking about it." Her hesitation may be rooted in fear or self-doubt. It may be based on a lack of faith; a perceived lack of energy, strength, or resources required for the task; or in simple laziness.

*"Exception" rebellion.* A third form of rebellion is saying to God, "I surrender all of my life to You, except this area." The area that remains unsurrendered is an expression of rebellion.

Every one of us has the potential for being rebellious in our thinking. Never assume you are too mature in your faith or too wise to fall into rebellion. Ask the Lord to reveal to you any area in which you remain stubbornly committed to doing things your way, even though you know your way is contrary to God's way, God's timing, or God's desire to have all of your life. (From *Finding Peace*, pages 85–86)

## A Letter to God

Not only is it important to come to the Lord fully confessing your negative thought patterns, it is also important that you confess to Him your very specific erroneous thoughts when it comes to God's nature, His Word, and the salvation He mercifully offers to us. It is very important that you acknowledge to God the rebellion of your heart and ask Him to forgive you of your rebellious thoughts and give you the courage and strength to repent of your rebellious behavior, changing the way you think, speak, and act.

Express to the Lord any doubts and reservations you have had about His love, the truth of His Word, or the assurance of your own salvation. Ask Him to help you to trust Him and to believe in Him, without doubt or rebellion.

## BREAKING THE PATTERNS OF BAD THINKING

You may be asking, *But how can I continuously think only about godly things?* You can't. You'd have to shut your eyes and ears and live in a vacuum not to respond with at least a passing thought to the ungodly perceptions, impressions, and words that are continually coming at you. But here's what you can do. You can refuse to allow negative impressions and images to lodge in your mind. You can refuse to dwell upon them, rehearse them, revisualize them, or embellish them in your imagination. You can refuse to pursue them, seeking "more of the same."

Any child of God who takes a willful stand against thought patterns that clearly are harmful is going to be provided a way of escape from that circumstance. God will help you focus your mind on something other than your problem or bad thought pattern if you will make the initial step in that direction. (From *Finding Peace*, pages 91–92)

### REFLECTION AND RESPONSE

Those who willfully choose to continue in a pattern of unproductive, bad thinking are those who willfully choose to estrange themselves from the Lord. We must use our will to choose to think as God would have us think. If we exert our will, God will endue us with His power so that we truly do have the willpower to change our thought patterns. As you read through the following verses, ask the Holy Spirit to reveal to you ways in which you might replace ungodly patterns of thinking with godly patterns of thinking.

1 CORINTHIANS 10:12–13~Therefore let him who thinks he stands take heed lest he fall. No temptation has overtaken you except such as is common to man; but God is faithful, who will not allow you to be tempted beyond what you are able, but with the temptation will also make the way of escape, that you may be able to bear it.

*General response:*

_____

_____

_____

_____

_____

*Personal response:*

_____

_____

_____

_____

ISAIAH 26:3~You will keep him in perfect peace,
                  Whose mind is stayed on You,
                  Because he trusts in You.

*General response:*

_____

_____

_____

_____

*Personal response:*

_____

_____

_____

_____

PHILIPPIANS 4:8–9~Finally, brethren, whatever things are true, whatever things are noble, whatever things are just, whatever things are pure, whatever things are lovely, whatever things are of good report, if there is any virtue and if there is anything praiseworthy—meditate on these things . . . and the God of peace will be with you.

*General response:*

_____

_____

_____

_____

*Personal response:*

_____

_____

_____

_____

∞

## DISCUSSION POINT

What are some very practical things you might do to change a negative, unproductive, or bad pattern of thinking into a pattern that is godly?

_____

_____

_____

_____

∞

## THANKS AND PRAISE

Now is a good time to offer thanksgiving and praise to God for His renewal of your mind, His cleansing of the thoughts of your heart, His healing of bad memories, and His power to help you develop a godly thought life. Identify at least ten things related to your "thinking" for which you can give thanks and praise to the Lord.

_____

_____

_____

_____

_____

_____

_____

_____

_____

# SEVEN

# LIVING WITHOUT REGRET

## KEY QUESTIONS TO ASK ABOUT REGRET

Any person who is feeling regret over his or her past needs to ask these five very important questions:

### 1. WAS THERE SOMETHING MORE I COULD HAVE DONE?

In any situation, there is usually a mix of things that a person can and can't do. If another person is involved in a situation, that mix can be very complicated.

One of the challenges we each face regarding regret is a sorting out of what was within the boundaries of our responsibility, power, ability, or decision-making choice. Some things are simply beyond our control, and those are things we should not feel guilty about.

If you have thoughts of *I should have . . . I ought to have . . .* or *I wish I had . . . ,* you are living with regret. The question you need to ask first is really this one: *Could I have?*

### 2. DID I FAIL TO TRUST GOD?

Regret in many people is rooted in the fact that they didn't have the courage, the strength, the fortitude, the resolve—and, most important, they didn't trust God to supply them with the courage, strength, fortitude, or resolve they needed. If you have trusted God in a situation to the best of your ability, lay down any guilt you feel. It's false guilt.

If you have not trusted God and have taken matters into your own hands, have rushed into decisions, or have acted in a way contrary to God's commandments, seek God's forgiveness.

### 3. DID I SIN?

Apart from mistakes and errors in timing, or poor choices, many people feel regret that stems from outright sin. In those cases, a person has willfully acted in a way that violates

God's commandments. There is no peace when that happens. The only solution when you are feeling regret over sin is to go to God and confess your sin, ask for His forgiveness, and then, on the basis of His Word, receive His forgiveness.

## 4. HAVE I FORGIVEN EVERYBODY INVOLVED IN THE SITUATION I REGRET, INCLUDING MYSELF?

Perhaps the most difficult part of forgiveness for many people is forgiving themselves. If God has forgiven you, you need to forgive yourself and go forward in your life. Don't continue to punish yourself over something that God has forgiven.

If God has forgiven you, you also need to forgive any person or group of people whom you believe to have been associated with the sin. Do not continue to dwell on them in your mind or heart. Let them go and trust God to deal with them in His way, in His timing.

## 5. DID I DENY OR TURN AWAY FROM GOD'S REVEALED WILL FOR MY LIFE?

Don't live in the regret of what "might have been" had you obeyed a specific call of God on your life in the past. There's no way of retracing those steps or regaining that opportunity.

Admit to God that you failed Him. Own up to the pride and selfish desires that were at the root of your decision to choose your way over His way. Ask God to forgive you and to lead you from this point onward. And then, as God reveals to you what He wants you to do now, obey Him. (From *Finding Peace*, pages 98–110)

## A Letter to God

As you read through the statements and questions above, did one or more of these issues related to regret stand out to you? I encourage you to take this opportunity to write a letter to God about things that you continue to feel regret about. Write to the Lord how you feel about what happened that you regret— ask Him to reveal to you if there was any sin on your part. Ask Him to reveal to you any way in which you failed to trust Him, failed to forgive others involved, or failed to pursue His revealed will for your life. When He does so, ask God for His forgiveness.

Include as part of your letter a statement of your renewed commitment to trust God in the future, and to obey what He says to you.

## GOD'S TOTAL FORGIVENESS, HEALING, AND RESTORATION

What God forgives, He forgives completely. What God heals, He brings to wholeness. What God restores, He does so without any limitations placed upon a person's potential for sharing the gospel and being a witness of God's love, mercy, and grace. (From *Finding Peace*, page 108)

### REFLECTION AND RESPONSE

Many people seem willing to accept that God forgives their sin, but they fail to recognize that what God forgives, God forgets. He forgives sin completely.

Many people seem willing to accept that God heals, but they fail to recognize that God seeks to bring a person to wholeness—which is a complete harmony of spirit, mind, body, and emotions.

Many people seem willing to accept that God can restore a person personally, but they fail to recognize that God desires to and seeks to completely restore a person to right relationships with all around him.

What God does in forgiving, healing, and restoring, He does to perfection and to the fullness of completion. We are the ones who have difficulty, at times, accepting the full magnitude of what God is capable of doing and what God desires to do in us.

As you read and reflect upon the following verses, keep these concepts of forgiveness, wholeness, and restoration in mind.

*Reflect upon and then respond to the verses below in both* general *and* personal *ways. Indicate what you believe to be the general message of these passages, and then identify what you believe the Lord has as a personal message to you.*

PSALM 103:12~As far as the east is from the west,
So far has He removed our transgressions from us.

*General response:*

_____

_____

_____

_____

*Personal response:*

_____

_____

_____

_____

PSALM 51:1–2, 7–8, 10,12~Have mercy upon me, O God,
According to Your lovingkindness;
According to the multitude of Your tender mercies,
Blot out my transgressions.
Wash me thoroughly from my iniquity,
And cleanse me from my sin . . .
Purge me with hyssop, and I shall be clean;
Wash me, and I shall be whiter than snow.
Make me hear joy and gladness . . .
Create in me a clean heart, O God,
And renew a steadfast spirit within me . . .
Restore to me the joy of Your salvation,
And uphold me by Your generous Spirit.

*General response:*

_____

_____

_____

_____

*Personal response:*

_____

_____

_____

_____

❦

## DISCUSSION POINT

How difficult is it for a person to accept that God has completely purged him or her of all sin, guilt, and shame?

How important is it that we receive God's full forgiveness and healing to the point that we once again "hear joy and gladness"?

_____

_____

_____

_____

2 CHRONICLES 7:14~If My people who are called by My name will humble themselves, and pray and seek My face, and turn from their wicked ways, then I will hear from heaven, and will forgive their sin and heal their land.

*General response:*

_____

_____

_____

_____

*Personal response:*

_____

_____

_____

_____

## Maintaining a Clear Conscience

The best way to live without regret is to maintain a clear conscience:

- Choose to live in such a way that you do your best in every task and in every relationship. Give your utmost and your best effort to live in a godly manner.

- Choose to trust God in every area of your life—every decision, every choice, every opportunity He sends your way.

- Choose to obey God. Keep His commandments.

- Choose to forgive others fully and freely.

- Choose to pursue what God reveals to you as His path for you to follow.

No person can do these things in his or her limited human power. But with the Holy Spirit residing in us, we can turn from all forms of temptation to pursue the good works that God has authorized us to do.

It is the Holy Spirit who works in us to

- prick our conscience if we are about to sin or have made a choice or decision that is going to lead us astray from God's perfect will for our lives.

- enable us to withstand and say no to a temptation.

- convict us of sin that we commit so we will turn immediately to the Lord and seek forgiveness.

- help us to pray and respond to life as we should, including prayer for others and forgiveness of others.

- show us the choices we are to make and the opportunities we are to pursue.

If you truly want to obey God's commandments and walk according to His principles for a godly life, your conscience is going to be tender—just a little prick from the Holy Spirit will cause you to turn away from sin. You will be quick to fall to your knees and seek God's forgiveness. If you have developed a rebellious heart and have chosen to walk according to your own self-made rules for living, your conscience is going to be callous. It will take a giant conviction from the Holy Spirit deep in your heart for you to want to deny the lustful plea-sures you desire and seek God's forgiveness for your sinful thoughts, words, or deeds.

The degree to which your conscience speaks to you is in direct relationship to the amount of rebellion in your heart and the number of times you have refused to do what the Holy Spirit has prompted you to do. (From *Finding Peace*, pages 112–115)

## REFLECTION AND RESPONSE

Living in a godly manner, trusting God, obeying God, forgiving others, and pursu-ing God's will for your life are all a matter of choice. God does not force us to love Him, trust Him, or obey Him. Rather, He empowers us and enables us to follow through on the choices we make to pursue a relationship with Him and to pursue His expressed will for our lives (as revealed in His Word and in our hearts by the power of the Holy Spirit). In contrast, God does not empower, honor, reward, or enable the choices we make that are rebellious, sinful, or neglectful of our rela-tionship with God. As you read and reflect on the verses below, keep the impor-tance of your own *willful choices* at the forefront of your thinking.

DEUTERONOMY 30:19–20~[Moses said:] "I call heaven and earth as witnesses today against you, that I have set before you life and death, blessing and cursing; therefore choose life, that both you and your descendants may live; that you may love the LORD your God, that you may obey His voice, and that you may cling to Him, for He is your life and the length of your days; and that you may dwell in the land which the LORD swore to your fathers, to Abraham, Isaac, and Jacob, to give them."

*General response:*

_____

_____

_____

_____

*Personal response:*

_____

_____

_____

_____

_____

JOSHUA 24:14–15~Now therefore, fear the LORD, serve Him in sincerity and in truth, and put away the gods which your fathers served on the other side of the River and in Egypt. Serve the LORD! And if it seems evil to you to serve the LORD, choose for yourselves this day whom you will serve, whether the gods which your fathers served that were on the other side of the River, or the gods of the Amorites, in whose land you dwell. But as for me and my house, we will serve the LORD.

*General response:*

_____

_____

_____

_____

*Personal response:*

_____

_____

_____

_____

JOHN 16:7–11~[Jesus said:] "Nevertheless I tell you the truth. It is to your advantage that I go away; for if I do not go away, the Helper will not come to you; but if I depart, I will send Him to you. And when He has come, He will convict the world of sin, and of righteousness, and of judgment: of sin, because they do not believe in Me; of righteousness, because I go to My Father and you see Me no more; of judgment, because the ruler of this world is judged."

*General response:*

_____

_____

_____

_____

*Personal response:*

_____

_____

_____

_____

∞

## Thanks and Praise

Now is a good time to give thanks and to offer your praise for the work of the Holy Spirit in you to help you maintain a good conscience. Using the statements provided above about the Holy Spirit's work, write out at least ten things related to the Holy Spirit's guidance for which you are thankful.

_____

_____

_____

_____

_____

_____

_____

_____

_____

_____

EIGHT

∞

# GIVING UP ANXIETY

## ARE YOU ANXIOUS, DISTRACTED, WORRIED?

Anxiety is a problem we all face at one time or another. The Greek word for "anxious" in the Sermon on the Mount means "distracted." It is a word that refers to uncertainty. That's what anxiety produces in us. It gives us a feeling of, *What next?* It is a feeling that the rug has been pulled out from under us and we have no idea if we are going to fall, how hard, in what direction, or onto what!

The word *anxious* is also translated as "worry" in the Bible. For many people, worry has become a way of life. They live in a state of uncertainty and worry. (From *Finding Peace*, pages 119–120)

### REFLECTION AND RESPONSE

Are you anxious or worried about something today? Are you uncertain about something? Identify some of your anxieties below:

- Is there a situation that has you feeling anxious or is there a relationship about which you feel uncertain?

  _____

  _____

  _____

- Is there a decision for which you can't seem to find an answer even though you know an answer is required and it will impact your future?

  _____

  _____

_____

_____

Read through the anxieties that you have identified. Next to each one of them, write in bold block letters, JESUS KNOWS . . . JESUS IS LORD.

So many times, our anxieties arise because we lose sight of the fact that God knows all about the situation, relationship, or decision that is related to our anxiety. He sees the beginning from the ending. As Lord over all, Jesus has authority over all spiritual principalities, powers, and dominions, as well as over all creation, all human beings (both individuals and institutions), and all systems of this world! Keep those truths in mind as you read and reflect on the following passages of Scripture.

MATTHEW 6:25–26~[Jesus said:] "Do not worry about your life, what you will eat or what you will drink; nor about your body, what you will put on. Is not life more than food and the body more than clothing? Look at the birds of the air, for they neither sow nor reap nor gather into barns; yet your heavenly Father feeds them. Are you not of more value than they?"

*General response:*

_____

_____

_____

_____

*Personal response:*

_____

_____

_____

_____

## Discussion Point

Note that Jesus *commanded* us not to worry. What are the consequences of our not obeying His command?

_____

_____

_____

_____

_____

_____

COLOSSIANS 2:6–10~As you therefore have received Christ Jesus the Lord, so walk in Him, rooted and built up in Him and established in the faith, as you have been taught, abounding in it with thanksgiving. Beware lest anyone cheat you through philosophy and empty deceit, according to the tradition of men, according to the basic principles of the world, and not according to Christ. For in Him dwells all the fullness of the Godhead bodily; and you are complete in Him, who is the head of all principality and power.

*General response:*

_____

_____

_____

_____

*Personal response:*

_____

_____

_____

_____

∽

## DISCUSSION POINT

How does this passage from Colossians negate the world's philosophy that being anxious is normal and to be expected? How does this passage negate the world's opinion that anxiety is a normal by-product of a world in which nuclear power, terrorism, and incurable diseases are *realities*?

_____

_____

_____

_____

## NO SITUATION AUTOMATICALLY CAUSES ANXIETY

No situation automatically causes anxiety. It certainly isn't God's purpose for you to feel anxious—He doesn't allow situations in your life so you will have anxiety. No! God may allow a situation in your life to help you to develop stronger faith, to grow and mature, or to change a bad habit or negative attitude. But God does not set you up for anxiety. He is always at work to bring you to a place where you will trust Him more, obey Him more fully, and receive more of His blessings.

We must be careful not to confuse concern with anxiety. It is normal for a Christian to have deep concerns. Concern motivates us to intercede and to take godly actions toward meeting the needs of others. Concern, yes! Anxiety, no!

Concern is rooted in caring. We are to be concerned, for example, about our families, our health, doing a good job in our work—because we care about the well-being of our families, our personal well-being, and the success of our work. Concern involves wanting to see things done well so that God receives glory from our lives.

Some concern is also rooted in obedience. There is no place in the Scriptures where we are given license to be irresponsible. We are to live out God's commandments in our daily lives. We are to live honest and moral lives—paying our bills, telling the truth, giving a full day's effort for a full day's wage, and so forth. Living a responsible life involves a certain amount of concern rooted in a desire to be obedient to the Lord.

A concern rooted in caring or in obedience, however, is not the same as anxiety. (From *Finding Peace*, pages 121–122)

## REFLECTION AND RESPONSE

Understanding the difference between concern and anxiety is very important. Many people say they are "concerned" when they are actually anxious. Try this simple exercise. Look at the words and phrases below and then write next to each one of them either *concern* or *anxiety*.

productive                        _____

paralyzes us                      _____

forward-looking                   _____

positive                          _____

a treadmill of fear               _____

motivates us to take action       _____

unproductive                      _____

stuck in the present              _____

leads us to make decisions        _____

rooted in trust of God            _____

Which set of characteristics describes the way you feel about a situation, relationship, or decision that you are facing? Is this what the Lord desires for you? If not, what *do* you believe He desires for you?

_____

_____

_____

_____

_____

## A Letter to God

Take a few minutes to write a letter to God about the anxiety you feel. Tell Him specifically how you feel. Express everything about the situation, relationship, or decision that causes any of the traits you have put in the *Anxiety* category above. Ask Him to give you a godly concern, but to remove anxiety from you.

## The Negative Results of Anxiety

Here are seven highly negative results associated with anxiety:

### 1. Anxiety Divides a Person's Mind

Many people live with a degree of stress that results from what I call a "divided mind." The person is working on one task, is engaged in a meeting with one group, or is involved in a conversation with one person, but in the back of that person's mind and heart, another problem or situation has center stage. A divided mind keeps a person from fully concentrating on the tasks at hand. Nagging worries or unsettling feelings distract him, causing him to live in a state of semiconfusion at all times.

### 2. Anxiety Lowers a Person's Productivity

If a person has a divided mind, it is only logical to conclude that such a person will be less productive. He won't be able to sustain an effort and will be less likely to see any project through to a quality completion. Not only is the person less productive, but he or she is usually less efficient too. The quality of work tends to suffer.

### 3. Anxiety Leads a Person to Make Unwise Decisions

The person who cannot focus on a task is a person who generally cannot complete his required "homework" on a project, cannot perceive all facets of a problem, and cannot listen at length or with sufficient concentration to those who might give sound advice. The result is often poor decision making and problem solving. Bad choices and decisions are a setup for failure, which only leads to greater anxiety.

### 4. Anxiety Drains a Person's Energy

Prolonged anxiety is exhausting. It wears out your immune system and alters certain chemical systems in your body so that you are depleted of vitamins and minerals that help you maintain a good energy level.

### 5. Anxiety Produces Physical Ailments

Anxiety produces numerous negative effects in the human body, including headaches, stomachaches, intestinal disorders, constriction of blood vessels resulting in high blood pressure and a greater likelihood of heart attacks and strokes, and biochemical disorders that put hormonal systems out of balance, which can result in multiple diseases.

## 6. ANXIETY ALIENATES OTHER PEOPLE

When a person is less focused or distracted, it becomes more difficult to communicate with him. Such a person often is fidgety and frustrated, quick to blame and to criticize others, and quick to become angry. Poor communication is very damaging to friendships, marriages, and parent-child relationships.

## 7. ANXIETY DEPLETES A PERSON'S JOY

The person who lives with prolonged anxiety is a person who usually feels robbed of joy.

Given all of these negative effects, our conclusion must be that a troubled soul is not God's plan for us! (From *Finding Peace*, pages 124–127)

### REFLECTION AND RESPONSE

Take the simple quiz below, indicating your response to each statement with an *X* in the column that reflects your current state of peace:

|  | TRUE | SOMETIMES | FALSE |
|---|---|---|---|
| 1. I have difficulty concentrating. | _____ | _____ | _____ |
| 2. I tend to be unfocused at times and can be easily distracted. | _____ | _____ | _____ |
| 3. I rarely sleep through the night. | _____ | _____ | _____ |
| 4. I am not as productive or efficient as I'd like to be; I'd like to produce higher-quality work than what I currently produce. | _____ | _____ | _____ |
| 5. I tend to make unwise decisions. | _____ | _____ | _____ |
| 6. I lack energy. | _____ | _____ | _____ |
| 7. I am not in great physical health. | _____ | _____ | _____ |
| 8. I tend to have headaches and stomachaches rather frequently. | _____ | _____ | _____ |
| 9. I wish I had more good, close, long-standing friendships. | _____ | _____ | _____ |
| 10. I am easily frustrated and tend to be fidgety. | _____ | _____ | _____ |

Take a look at the general pattern you have made with your *X* responses. If your *X* responses tend to be toward the "True" and "Sometimes" side, you very likely have an anxiety problem!

"But," you may say, "anxiety isn't really a sin." The truth is, God has commanded us, "Do not fret!" There are countless examples in Scripture that tell us God desires for us to have focused minds and productive lives. God desires for us to make wise decisions. God desires for us to have close, meaningful relationships and open, transparent communication with the people around us. He desires for us to have an abundance of joy!

Reflect upon and respond to the verses below, noting especially any words or phrases that seem to stand out to you. Ask the Holy Spirit what He may be trying to communicate to you!

PSALM 37:8~Do not fret—it only causes harm.

*General response:*

_____

_____

_____

_____

_____

_____

*Personal response:*

_____

_____

_____

_____

_____

_____

∽

## DISCUSSION POINT

How much time and energy are spent by some people today worrying about what they will eat, drink, and wear?

What are some strategies a person can adopt to *stop* worrying about food, drink, and clothing?

_____

_____

_____

_____

_____

PROVERBS 16:3~Commit your works to the LORD,

And your thoughts will be established.

*General response:*

_____

_____

_____

_____

*Personal response:*

_____

_____

_____

_____

## DEALING WITH ANXIETY

What should we do when anxiety strikes? First and foremost, we must ask God to give us His peace and His answers. Very specifically, we must ask God to deal with the problems that are filling both our conscious and subconscious minds. This is not likely something we do just once. It is something we may have to do many times throughout the day.

We must ask the Lord to help us focus all of our thoughts and energy on the immediate situation at hand.

You can fall into a downward spiral of anxiety. Or you can say, "Heavenly Father! I bring this to You. It's beyond my control or influence. I feel helpless in this situation, but You have the power to change it. You love me perfectly. I am trusting You to handle this in the way You see fit. I know that whatever You have planned for me is for my good. I look forward to seeing the way You choose to express Your love and wisdom and power." (From *Finding Peace*, pages 128–131)

NINE

&#x221e;

# GETTING TO THE ROOT CAUSES
# OF PROLONGED ANXIETY

## ADDRESSING THE CAUSES OF LONG-TERM ANXIETY

People have told me from time to time, "I'm just a worrier." Or they have told me about someone they know well, "He's always a little uptight," or "She tends to fret a lot." Some people refer to this continually anxious state as being "high-strung" or "always wound tight." If a state of anxiety has become the norm for your life, however, you need to take a look at the reasons for that feeling. They are generally related to deep inner needs. Those needs tend to relate to one or more of the following.

### 1. A LACK OF SELF-WORTH

A person who feels a lack of self-worth has lost sight of his or her value to God, our heavenly Father. Jesus sacrificed Himself for you and me. Nothing God could ever do would be a greater display of the truth that He considers you to be worthy of loving, nurturing, and blessing.

### 2. A DESIRE FOR TOTAL CONTROL

A second deep inner cause of anxiety is a desire to control all things to our benefit, including things over which we truly have no power. I believe this desire for power and control often springs from a lack of trust in God, who alone can control every aspect of our lives.

### 3. CONCERN FOR WHAT OTHERS THINK

Jesus tells us that our heavenly Father's opinion about who we are is all that truly matters. If He approves of us, that's all the approval we need. He gives us our identity and an inner beauty that far surpass anything related to what we might wear, own, drive, or live in.

## 4. STRIVING TO FOLLOW THE WORLD'S PATTERN

The world tells us that we will feel secure if we just get our house mortgage fully paid, if we just follow a certain health regimen, if we are promoted to a position that's high enough in the company or we achieve a certain degree of fame. The truth is that the world has no magic solution for 100 percent security in any area of life. Only Jesus can give a person the confidence of security deep within.

## 5. LIVING IN THE TOMORROW

One of the foremost causes of anxiety is a desire for the good things of the future to arrive. Friend, the God who is in control of today is also the God who is fully in control of tomorrow. He has already prepared for what will happen to you! He has already provided what you will need tomorrow. He has already anticipated the problems you will face tomorrow and set into motion everything required to resolve those problems. (From *Finding Peace*, pages 133–141)

### REFLECTION AND RESPONSE

As you read through the above statement, did you find yourself saying about any one of these five causes of long-term anxiety, "I feel that way"? If so, face up to the fact that you may be harboring long-term anxiety in your heart. You must address that and deal with it if you truly are going to live in a state of peace.

A number of verses in the Bible address the issues of self-worth, a desire for control, concern for what others think, striving to follow the world's patterns, and living in the tomorrow. If you find yourself dealing with one particular cause of anxiety, I encourage you to use a concordance and study more on that area in God's Word. God has answers for you!

MATTHEW 6:26~Look at the birds of the air, for they neither sow nor reap nor gather into barns; yet your heavenly Father feeds them. Are you not of more value than they?

*General response:*

_____

_____

_____

_____

*Personal response:*

_____

_____

_____

PSALM 24:1–2~The earth is the LORD'S, and all its fullness,

        The world and those who dwell therein.

        For He has founded it upon the seas,

        And established it upon the waters.

*General response:*

_____

_____

_____

_____

*Personal response:*

_____

_____

_____

_____

MATTHEW 6:33–34~[Jesus said:] "Seek first the kingdom of God and His righteousness, and all these things shall be added to you. Therefore do not worry about
tomorrow, for tomorrow will worry about its own things. Sufficient for the day is
its own trouble."

*General response:*

_____

_____

_____

_____

*Personal response:*

_____

_____

_____

_____

## DISCUSSION POINT

How important is it that we become free of long-term anxiety in order to live in
God's peace?

_____

_____

_____

_____

## A Letter to God

Take this opportunity to write a letter to God addressing any long-term anxiety
you may have. Tell Him about your feelings of low self-worth, your concerns about
the opinions of others and about conforming to the systems of the world, your
need to exert control in every situation, or your tendency to live in anticipation of

the future. Ask the Lord to set you free from the anxiety that lies deep within your heart.

_____

_____

_____

_____

_____

_____

_____

_____

_____

_____

_____

_____

_____

_____

_____

_____

_____

_____

_____

_____

## A Grievance Statement

Were you raised by parents who loved you conditionally? Are you perhaps in a marriage with a person who loves you conditionally? Conditional love says, "I love you *if* . . ." Expressions of love are bestowed in exchange for desired behavior.

Those who live in close relationship with those who love conditionally can have a very deep feeling of anxiety. They never know fully what they should be doing or saying in order to warrant the love of a person who is very important to them. If you are striving to win the love of a person who loves conditionally, you will always be disappointed and frustrated to some degree. It's time to face up to the nature of this relationship and to express to God the hurts and frustrations you have felt. If you are truly honest with yourself, you likely are harboring considerable resentment, bitterness, and anger toward those who have given or are giving you conditional love.

In this grievance statement, you are likely to find that the more you write, the more you have to write. Identify the person or people who taught you to love conditionally. Recognize that the enemy of your soul does not want you to experience the unconditional love of the Lord.

Use the space provided here or write out your grievance statement on a separate sheet of paper.

_____

_____

_____

_____

_____

_____

_____

_____

_____

_____

_____

_____

_____

_____

_____

_____

_____

_____

_____

_____

_____

_____

_____

As you bring your grievance statement before the Lord, ask Him to set you free from long-term anxiety. Express aloud a statement of your trust that He will do so!

## GOD'S DESIRE TO FREE US FROM LONG-TERM ANXIETY

God desires that we view our troubles, whether present concerns or those looming in the future, from His perspective. We are not to deny them or seek to escape them, but rather to regard them as trials and tribulations that we must overcome.

God never expects us to put up with constant anxiety. He intends for us to confront those situations that make us anxious, to face up to the anxiety we have allowed to fill our hearts, and to come to grips with the agitation we feel inside. He intends for us to resist the tendency to worry or become fearful and to refuse to lay down our peace no matter what the devil sends our way. (From *Finding Peace*, page 142)

### REFLECTION AND RESPONSE

The Bible speaks repeatedly about the "rest" that the Lord provides to His people. The meaning of this word *rest* in the Bible includes the concepts of "freedom from oppression by enemies" and "peace of spirit," not just a physical rest. It is a term that refers to total trust in the Lord. As you read through the verses below, note any words or phrases that stand out to you in a special way. What is the Lord speaking to you about His desire for you to come to a place of "rest" in Him?

PSALM 55:4–7, 16–18, 22~My heart is severely pained within me,
　　　　　　　　　And the terrors of death have fallen upon me.
　　　　　　　　　Fearfulness and trembling have come upon me,
　　　　　　　　　And horror has overwhelmed me.
　　　　　　　　　So I said, "Oh, that I had wings like a dove!
　　　　　　　　　I would fly away and be at rest.
　　　　　　　　　Indeed, I would wander far off,
　　　　　　　　　And remain in the wilderness . . .
　　　　　　　　　As for me, I will call upon God,
　　　　　　　　　And the LORD shall save me.
　　　　　　　　　Evening and morning and at noon
　　　　　　　　　I will pray, and cry aloud,
　　　　　　　　　And He shall hear my voice.

> He has redeemed my soul in peace from the battle that
>      was against me,
> For there were many against me . . .
> Cast your burden on the LORD,
> And He shall sustain you;
> He shall never permit the righteous to be moved.

*General response:*

_____

_____

_____

_____

*Personal response:*

_____

_____

_____

_____

MATTHEW 11:28–30~[Jesus said:] "Come to Me, all you who labor and are heavy laden, and I will give you rest. Take My yoke upon you and learn from Me, for I am gentle and lowly in heart, and you will find rest for your souls. For My yoke is easy and My burden is light."

*General response:*

_____

_____

_____

_____

*Personal response:*

_____

_____

_____

_____

❧

## DISCUSSION POINT

What do you believe is required on your part as a prerequisite for leaving behind long-term anxieties and entering into the rest that the Lord has for you?

_____

_____

_____

_____

❧

## THANKS AND PRAISE

Now is a good time to thank and praise the Lord for all that He does to free us from the bondage of long-term anxiety. In the space below, identify at least ten attributes of the Lord or examples of His goodness to you through the years in giving you a deep sense of self-worth, freeing you from feeling as if you have to exert control over all things, freeing you from needing the approval of others at all times, freeing you from feeling bound to the systems and expectations of the world, and freeing you from worry about the future.

_____

_____

_____

_____

_____

_____

_____

_____

_____

_____

# TEN

∞

# LIVING IN PEACE WITH OTHERS

## THE CHALLENGE OF LIVING IN PEACE WITH OTHERS

It seems almost inevitable that we all will have neighbors or acquaintances who are not easy to get along with. Some of them would probably say the same about us. Nevertheless, we are encouraged to do all that we can to live peacefully with all men and women.

The implication is that it is not going to be possible in all situations to be at peace with every person. God knows our human nature. He knows that we will be at odds with people from time to time, even other followers of Jesus who are our brothers and sisters in the faith. His challenge to us is this: Don't let the fault for a lack of peace be the result of something *you* have done. (From *Finding Peace*, page 144)

### REFLECTION AND RESPONSE

During the last several years of his life, the apostle Paul lived in various degrees of confinement or imprisonment. He was chained for a time between two Roman soldiers. His personal situation was far from peaceful. Even so, it was during this period that Paul wrote most powerfully about living in peace with others, even our enemies. As you read through the following verses, reflect on what it means to live in peace with your Christian brothers and sisters, as well as what it means to live in peace with those who do not serve the Lord and who actually may consider you to be an enemy. Be sensitive to key words and phrases that the Holy Spirit may call to your attention. Ask the Lord to reveal to you what He desires to teach you.

*Reflect upon and then respond to the verses below in both* general *and* personal *ways. Indicate what you believe to be the general message of these passages, and then identify what you believe the Lord has as a personal message to you.*

ROMANS 12:18–19~If it is possible, as much as depends on you, live peaceably with all men. Beloved, do not avenge yourselves, but rather give place to wrath; for it is written, "Vengeance is Mine, I will repay," says the Lord.

*General response:*

_____

_____

_____

_____

*Personal response:*

_____

_____

_____

_____

EPHESIANS 4:1–7~I, therefore, the prisoner of the Lord, beseech you to walk worthy of the calling with which you were called, with all lowliness and gentleness, with longsuffering, bearing with one another in love, endeavoring to keep the unity of the Spirit in the bond of peace. There is one body and one Spirit, just as you were called in one hope of your calling; one Lord, one faith, one baptism; one God and Father of all, who is above all, and through all, and in you all. But to each one of us grace was given according to the measure of Christ's gift.

*General response:*

_____

_____

_____
_____
_____

*Personal response:*

_____
_____
_____
_____

## Discussion Point

How do you respond to Ephesians 4:7~ "To each one of us grace was given according to the measure of Christ's gift"? What does Christ's death on the cross and the eternal gift of salvation really mean to you? How does it enable you to live in peace with others?

_____
_____
_____
_____

PHILIPPIANS 2:1–2~Therefore if there is any consolation in Christ, if any comfort of love, if any fellowship of the Spirit, if any affection and mercy, fulfill my joy by being like-minded, having the same love, being of one accord, of one mind.

*General response:*

_____
_____
_____
_____

*Personal response:*

_____

_____

_____

_____

∽

## DISCUSSION POINT

What do these verses say to you about the currently popular term *tolerance?* To what extent are we to be true to the gospel of Jesus Christ?

How important is it that we remain in the "consolation in Christ" and the "fellowship of the Spirit" in order to be able to do what these passages command us to do?

_____

_____

_____

_____

## GETTING RID OF A SELF-FIRST ATTITUDE

Pride is difficult to lay down. It is at the core of our person. It is not our normal human instinct to be selfless, giving, or generous toward others. That instinct of "self first" isn't automatically removed when we become Christians. God does not remove self or pride from any of us as if by some spiritual surgery. Self-focused pride is something that we must lay down, give up, or yield to the Lord. Learning to serve others, to lay down our lives for others, is a principle clearly taught in the Scriptures, but it is never taught as though it were an easy lesson to learn. (From *Finding Peace,* pages 145–146)

### REFLECTION AND RESPONSE

The Bible has a great deal to say about pride and selfishness. As you read through these few verses below, take special note of any word or phrase that seems to stand out to you in a special way. What do you believe the Lord is saying to you?

1 JOHN 2:16–17~For all that is in the world—the lust of the flesh, the lust of the eyes, and the pride of life—is not of the Father but is of the world. And the world is passing away, and the lust of it; but he who does the will of God abides forever.

*General response:*

_____

_____

_____

_____

*Personal response:*

_____

_____

_____

_____

OBADIAH 3–4~"The pride of your heart has deceived you,

       You who dwell in the clefts of the rock,

       Whose habitation is high;

       You who say in your heart, 'Who will bring me down to the ground?'

       Though you ascend as high as the eagle,

       And though you set your nest among the stars,

       From there I will bring you down," says the LORD.

*General response:*

_____

_____

_____

_____

*Personal response:*

_____

_____

_____

_____

PROVERBS 13:10~By pride comes nothing but strife,
                    But with the well-advised is wisdom.

*General response:*

_____

_____

_____

_____

*Personal response:*

_____

_____

_____

_____

∞

## DISCUSSION POINT

Pride *always* produces strife, and ultimately a "fall" from the blessings and goodness of God—not only in our individual lives but in any church group. What is the difference between pride and confidence?

_____

_____

_____

_____

In what ways are we to come against a proud spirit in our personal lives?

_____

_____

_____

_____

PHILIPPIANS 2:3–4~Let nothing be done through selfish ambition or conceit, but in lowliness of mind let each esteem others better than himself. Let each of you look out not only for his own interests, but also for the interests of others.

*General response:*

_____

_____

_____

_____

*Personal response:*

_____

_____

_____

_____

## DISCUSSION POINT

How much more do you perceive might be done in your church if every person looked out for the interests of others and had no "selfish ambition or conceit"?

_____

_____

_____

_____

_____

_____

# SURFACE ISSUES THAT CAN CAUSE CONFLICT

Pride runs deep, but there are a number of other issues that are more on the surface, that can be destructive to peace and cause conflict in our lives. The difference is that pride *automatically* results in conflict. These surface issues do not *need* to produce conflict. They cause conflict only because we allow them to do so. These are issues that can be resolved or curtailed in such a way that they do not become divisive.

## 1. PERSONALITY CONFLICTS

Certainly not all of us are alike, have the same style, enjoy the same things, think, or act alike. We do have differences in our personalities. But a personality conflict should never erupt in a feud or a war. A personality conflict is not a good reason to shut out another person, criticize him, or seek vengeance against him. Admit that you are different as human beings. Be kind and courteous, and go on down the road. Seek out people whose company you enjoy. But don't shut a door of ministry or refuse to help another person just because you don't like his personality.

## 2. DIFFERENCES IN OPINION

What holds true for personality conflicts also holds true for those who have differences of opinion. We don't necessarily need to agree with others on every point of every issue in order to have a productive, meaningful, enjoyable, and purposeful relationship with that person.

## 3. DIFFERENCES IN STYLE AND METHODOLOGY

From time to time you are going to encounter people you like, and who believe as you do, but who disagree with you over a particular approach, decision-making protocol, methodology, or style choice. Differences in methodology are no cause for frustration, hatred, anger, or division.

## 4. COMMUNICATION ERRORS

On occasion, we experience distress because of a failure to communicate well. Sometimes people don't state their positions or directions clearly, or hear accurately what is being said. So often we hear what we want to hear.

*What about anger in conversation?* Let me quickly point out that angry eruptions are not a godly communication style. If a person has a hot temper, he needs to recognize that he doesn't have true peace deep inside.

*Are you misinterpreting?* Sometimes it is easy to become upset and lose our peace when we feel we have been misunderstood. Do you ever feel rejection when somebody voices something that you interpret as criticism? It is not easy, but if you are committed to living at peace with others, be willing to recognize that it is not difficult to misread the intent of other people's words and actions. (From *Finding Peace*, pages 147–154)

## REFLECTION AND RESPONSE

The Bible has a number of verses that deal with the four issues I have identified above as *surface* issues. If you found yourself saying about any one of these issues, "I think that is at the heart of my conflict with a person," I encourage you to use a concordance and get more of God's wisdom on that particular issue.

Reflect upon and respond to the following verses, asking the Holy Spirit to show you not only what may be divisive in one or more relationships in your life, but also to reveal to you how you should respond right now to bring God's healing to that relationship. What action can you take to move beyond the things that divide you and find a way of working together for the greater good of the gospel?

EPHESIANS 4:25–32; 5:1–2~Therefore, putting away lying, "Let each one of you speak truth with his neighbor," for we are members of one another. "Be angry, and do not sin": do not let the sun go down on your wrath, nor give place to the devil. Let him who stole steal no longer, but rather let him labor, working with his hands what is good, that he may have something to give him who has need. Let no corrupt word proceed out of your mouth, but what is good for necessary edification, that it may impart grace to the hearers. And do not grieve the Holy Spirit of God, by whom you were sealed for the day of redemption. Let all bitterness, wrath, anger, clamor, and evil speaking be put away from you, with all malice. And be kind to one another, tenderhearted, forgiving one another, even as God in Christ forgave you.

Therefore be imitators of God as dear children. And walk in love, as Christ also has loved us and given Himself for us, an offering and a sacrifice to God for a sweet-smelling aroma.

*General response:*

_____

_____

_____

_____

*Personal response:*

_____

_____

_____

_____

PHILIPPIANS 2:14–16~Do all things without complaining and disputing, that you may become blameless and harmless, children of God without fault in the midst of a crooked and perverse generation, among whom you shine as lights in the world, holding fast the word of life, so that I may rejoice in the day of Christ that I have not run in vain or labored in vain.

*General response:*

_____

_____

_____

*Personal response:*

_____

_____

_____

## A Grievance Statement

As you have read through the statement about surface issues, and the preceding Bible verses, have you found yourself thinking about a specific relationship? Have you been holding something in your heart against a person who may have erupted in anger against you, misinterpreted you, or had strong differences with you regarding opinions, methodology, or issues of style? This is your opportunity to express all that you feel about that person to the Lord! As you finish writing your grievance statement below, or on another sheet of paper, ask the Lord to help you forgive this person—to set them free from your mind and heart.

_____

_____

_____

_____

_____

_____

_____

_____

_____

_____

_____

_____

_____

_____

## AN OPPORTUNITY TO GROW IN CHRIST

Fiery-dart comments hurt. They wound us. There's no escaping them, and no escaping the wounding they cause unless we totally shut ourselves off from other people, which isn't what God desires for us. No, these moments are opportunities for us to experience the power and presence of God in our lives, which can enable us to have peace in the midst of persecution.

Jesus said that we are blessed when people say evil things against us *falsely*. If there's truth in the criticism that is flung your way, don't turn your back on that truth. Take it to heart and ask God how He would have you change your attitude or behavior. There's no blessing in doing something that is an error, sin, or act of unrighteousness, then ignoring or denying what you have done. There's blessing only in what you do that is good and right before God.

Second, Jesus said we are blessed if people speak evil against us falsely *for His sake*. Blessing comes to us when we are living out what God has called us to do, and when others criticize us for heeding *His* words and obeying *His* plan and purpose for our lives. (From *Finding Peace*, page 156)

### REFLECTION AND RESPONSE

As you reflect upon and respond to the verses below, ask the Lord to reveal to you whether you have been falsely accused or if you have been accused *for the Lord's sake*. Ask the Lord to show you any incident in which you have simply reaped the consequences of your own bad choices or behavior. Be quick to confess your sin to the Lord and to ask the Lord to help you change your attitude, speech, or actions.

MATTHEW 5:11–12~[Jesus said:] "Blessed are you when they revile and persecute you, and say all kinds of evil against you falsely for My sake. Rejoice and be exceedingly glad, for great is your reward in heaven."

*General response:*

_____

_____

_____

_____

*Personal response:*

_____

_____

_____

_____

MARK 11:25–26~[Jesus taught:] "Whenever you stand praying, if you have any-thing against anyone, forgive him, that your Father in heaven may also forgive you your trespasses. But if you do not forgive, neither will your Father in heaven forgive your trespasses."

*General response:*

_____

_____

_____

_____

*Personal response:*

_____

_____

_____

_____

LUKE 17:1–4~[Jesus said:] "It is impossible that no offenses should come, but woe to him through whom they do come! It would be better for him if a millstone were hung around his neck, and he were thrown into the sea, than that he should offend one of these little ones. Take heed to yourselves. If your brother sins against you, rebuke him; and if he repents, forgive him. And if he sins against you seven times in a day, and seven times in a day returns to you, saying, 'I repent,' you shall forgive him."

*General response:*

_____

_____

_____

_____

*Personal response:*

_____

_____

_____

_____

## A Letter to God

As you have read through this chapter, have you felt a particular concern or "heaviness" in your spirit about one or more relationships in your life? Have you perhaps been holding a negative or hurtful encounter or conversation in your mind, dwelling on it repeatedly? Do you feel you have been treated unjustly by a person you love or who is in authority over you? This is your opportunity to write a letter to God about those troublesome encounters and difficult relationships. Express yourself fully, being very specific about the hurt you feel and the anger, resentment, or bitterness you may have been harboring in your heart. Ask the Lord to cleanse you of any fault on your part, and to show you what you might do to bring about reconciliation, healing, or restoration in the relationship that has been bruised or broken.

ELEVEN

∞

# RESTORING PEACE IN RELATIONSHIPS

## TAKING RESPONSIBILITY FOR YOUR ACTIONS

Our salvation does not automatically keep us from being mean, jealous, hateful, or angry. It is only as we ask the Holy Spirit to work in us and through us, only as we yield our nature to His nature, only as we seek to be His representatives on this earth in every relationship we have, that we are going to move beyond pride into the behaviors that establish peace.

So often people aren't willing to take responsibility for their actions. When a dispute arises, many people settle into the excuse "I can't help it. That's just the way I am." It never dawns on them that they can *change* the way they are, or that God desires for them to do just that! Choosing the right course of action, especially one that may cause us to lose face or feel shame for our part in a dispute, is probably the last thing we want to do, but it is the foundation stone of being at peace with others. It is the *heart* of the matter. I focus on the word *heart* because it is key to being at peace. (From *Finding Peace*, pages 159–160)

### REFLECTION AND RESPONSE

As I have indicated in the statement above, taking responsibility for your part in any dispute is essential not only to restoring peace in a damaged relationship with another person, but it is important for identifying any patterns of "poor relating" you may have in your own personal life. Do you find that things go wrong repeatedly in your friendships, that the same arguments and disputes seem to arise over and over in your marriage, or that you are in repeated conflict with your coworkers or supervisor on the job? A pattern of "poor relating" may have taken root.

Below, focus on one incident in which you ended up in conflict with another person.

## A CONFLICT INCIDENT

Who was involved?
When did this occur?
Where did this occur?
What was said or done?
What seemed to trigger the dispute or conflict?

Did the conflict escalate—did it grow, become more widespread, or spill over into other events or conversations?

_____

_____

_____

What was *your* part in the initial *triggering* of the dispute or conflict?

_____

_____

_____

What was *your* part in the *escalation* or ongoing life of the dispute or conflict?

_____

_____

_____

_____

Was the conflict or dispute resolved? *Temporarily* or *permanently*? (Some disputes or conflicts are glossed over for the sake of a temporary truce, but are never permanently healed. If a conflict is not definitively healed, it can continue to fester just below the surface, sometimes for years and even decades.)

_____

_____

_____

_____

Even if you do not believe you had any part in the initial triggering of a dispute or conflict, if the conflict escalated or continued, there was a role you played in allowing this to happen. It is very important that you be honest with yourself about this because what happened in this one incident is much more likely to happen in future relationships if you do not identify the role you played.

　　Has an incident such as the one above occurred more than once with this same person? Has an incident such as this occurred with other people?

_____

_____

_____

_____

The Bible has a number of verses that deal with a *contentious* person—a person prone to conflict or argument. Related concepts are *strife, strivings,* and *disputes.* As you read and reflect upon the selected passages below, be open to ways in which the Holy Spirit may call your attention to a particular phrase or word.

PROVERBS 17:14~The beginning of strife is like releasing water;
　　　　　　　Therefore stop contention before a quarrel starts.

*General response:*

_____

_____

_____

_____

*Personal response:*

_____

_____

_____

_____

PROVERBS 18:6–7~A fool's lips enter into contention,
      And his mouth calls for blows.
      A fool's mouth is his destruction,
      And his lips are the snare of his soul.

*General response:*

_____

_____

_____

_____

*Personal response:*

_____

_____

_____

_____

TITUS 3:9–11~Avoid foolish disputes, genealogies, contentions, and strivings about the law; for they are unprofitable and useless. Reject a divisive man after the first and second admonition, knowing that such a person is warped and sinning, being self-condemned.

*General response:*

_____

_____

_____

_____

*Personal response:*

_____

_____

_____

_____

_____

## DISCUSSION POINT

What is the difference between presenting the argument for Christ—counteracting lies and false philosophies with the truth of the gospel—and entering into disputes or strife?

_____

_____

_____

_____

_____

_____

_____

_____

_____

_____

_____

_____

## A Grievance Statement

Is there a particular person who seems to have identified you as his or her enemy, to the point that he or she continually seeks to "pick a fight" with you? Use this opportunity to write a grievance statement against this person or group. You may use the space provided below or your own sheet of paper.

_____

_____

_____

_____

_____

_____

_____

_____

_____

_____

_____

_____

_____

_____

_____

_____

---

_____

_____

_____

_____

_____

_____

_____

_____

_____

_____

_____

_____

_____

_____

_____

_____

As you bring this statement before the Lord, ask the Lord to show you how best to deal with this persecution. Ask the Lord to do *His* part in dealing with those who oppose you repeatedly. Ask the Lord to cleanse you of any unrighteous actions or words, and to help you always to deal with your persecutors in a godly manner. Pray that God will act decisively and quickly on your behalf!

# Having a Heart for Peace

God is the ultimate answer to any difficulties you may have in the area of dispute or conflict with others. What is the first thing you should do if you find that you are unable to resolve a difference or reconcile a disagreement in peace? Go to God with the problem. Go to God's Word. As you seek God's directives, give yourself a heart check. See if you have . . .

## 1. A PURE HEART

Those with a pure heart desire what God desires more than what they personally want.

## 2. A LOVING HEART

Loving is always expressed by giving. At times, the greatest act of love may be a gift of forgiveness, or it may be godly advice or admonition. It may be the gift of an encouraging word or genuine compliment. It may be a gift that meets a specific need for security, comfort, health, or provision in another person's life. A loving heart always looks toward the highest and greatest expression of God's love in a relationship. It is love that is unconditional and overflowing.

## 3. A PATIENT HEART

We are to be patient with the other person in a relationship, giving God time to work in his or her life. We must be willing to endure some tough times, some criticism, and even some times when we may not be able to discern clearly what God is doing.

## 4. A FORGIVING HEART

Forgiveness means that we are willing to let go of the pain we feel, and give it to God. We are willing to place every hurt and injustice into the hands of God and trust Him to heal our hearts and deal with those who have wounded us.

We must *always* forgive. There is never any situation in which unforgiveness can be justified before God. Forgiveness does not mean that we deny our injury, dismiss our pain, or lay aside all claims to justice. It *does* mean that we must release that person from our own judgment and let go of any bitterness or feelings of revenge. (From *Finding Peace*, pages 160–163)

## REFLECTION AND RESPONSE

How pure, loving, patient, and forgiving are you? Below is an opportunity to be brutally honest with yourself! The way you "feel" or perceive yourself to be may *not* be the way others see you! Put an *X* only in those spaces where you have full assurance that you are correctly evaluating your attitude and behavior. Put an *O* in those spaces where you have doubt or where you know that you and others do *not* see you as having the attribute identified.

| | I SEE MYSELF THIS WAY | MY FAMILY AND FRIENDS SEE ME THIS WAY | TOTAL STRANGERS SEE ME THIS WAY |
| --- | --- | --- | --- |
| 1. I am a pure person. | _____ | _____ | _____ |
| 2. I am a loving person. | _____ | _____ | _____ |
| 3. I am a patient person. | _____ | _____ | _____ |
| 4. I am a forgiving person. | _____ | _____ | _____ |

The Bible addresses our need for a pure, loving, patient, and forgiving heart in numerous verses, only a few of which are provided below. As you reflect upon these verses, note especially any words or phrases that stand out to you in a special way. Ask the Lord to give you a "heart checkup."

MARK 9:49–50~[Jesus taught:] "Everyone will be seasoned with fire, and every sacrifice will be seasoned with salt. Salt is good, but if the salt loses its flavor, how will you season it? Have salt in yourselves, and have peace with one another."

*General response:*

_____

_____

_____

_____

NOTE: Salt was the purest substance known to man at the time Jesus spoke these words. It came from the purest sources in the natural world—the sea and sun.

Salt become impure and lost its saltiness if it was exposed to pollutants in the air or earth. In a spiritual sense, sin is the ultimate impurity that destroys our saltiness.

*Personal response:*

_____

_____

_____

_____

COLOSSIANS 3:12–13~Put on tender mercies, kindness, humility, meekness, long-suffering; bearing with one another, and forgiving one another.

*General response:*

_____

_____

_____

_____

NOTE: To be long-suffering means to be patient.

*Personal response:*

_____

_____

_____

_____

## DISCUSSION POINT

What does it mean to have salt in yourselves? (See Mark 9:49–50 above. Also, you may want to refer to Matthew 5:13 and James 3:12.)

_____

_____

_____

_____

## A Letter to God

Have you felt convicted at some point in your reflection upon the preceding statement and verses that you may *not* have the pure, loving, patient, and forgiving heart
that God desires for you to have? Now is your time to write a letter to God about
this. Express to Him the struggle you may have in remaining pure, loving, and
patient. Express to Him how difficult it is for you to forgive some people—perhaps
even one person in particular. Ask the Lord to help you, by the power and presence
of His Holy Spirit, to develop a heart that truly is directed toward peace. Ask Him
to give you a desire to develop a pure, loving, patient, and forgiving spirit.

_____

_____

_____

_____

_____

_____

_____

_____

_____

_____

_____

## WHAT GOD REQUIRES OF YOU

Should the other person decide to walk away from your relationship, you are not responsible for his action. Should the other person decide to leave your employment, you are not responsible for her decision. Should the other person decide to continue to treat you with contempt, criticism, condemnation, or cruel behavior, you are not responsible for his behavior.

Do all that you know to do to live in peace with others—with a pure, loving, patient, and forgiving heart—and you will have done what God requires of you. This foundation, then, prepares you for any situation in which broken relationships are threatening to capsize your boat. (From *Finding Peace*, page 163)

### REFLECTION AND RESPONSE

Have you ever struggled with wondering if you did or are doing everything possible to restore or reconcile a relationship? If you have dealt with the person in a pure, loving, patient, and forgiving manner, you are standing on a firm foundation that makes restoration or reconciliation possible. You cannot, however, dictate another person's actions, and you are not responsible for the willful choices they may make. Your struggle may be a lack of forgiving yourself after you have requested and received God's forgiveness. On the other hand, if you have not dealt with the person in a pure, loving, patient, and forgiving manner, there's good cause for you to confess your "heart failure" to the Lord and ask His forgiveness. Also ask the Lord to help you begin right now to relate to the person in a pure, loving, patient, and forgiving manner.

Reflect on the following verses, asking the Holy Spirit to free you, heal you, restore you, and reconcile your relationships according to God's Word. Take special note of some specific directives as you attempt to live out purity, love, patience, and forgiveness in a relationship.

1 TIMOTHY 4:12~Let no one despise your youth, but be an example to the believers in word, in conduct, in love, in spirit, in faith, in purity.

*General response:*

_____

_____

_____

_____

*Personal response:*

_____

_____

_____

_____

2 CORINTHIANS 6:3–11~We give no offense in anything, that our ministry may not be blamed. But in all things we commend ourselves as ministers of God: in much patience, in tribulations, in needs, in distresses, in stripes, in imprisonments, in tumults, in labors, in sleeplessness, in fastings; by purity, by knowledge, by longsuffering, by kindness, by the Holy Spirit, by sincere love, by the word of truth, by the power of God, by the armor of righteousness on the right hand and on the left, by honor and dishonor, by evil report and good report; as deceivers, and yet true; as unknown, and yet well known; as dying, and behold we live; as chastened, and yet not killed; as sorrowful, yet always rejoicing; as poor, yet making many rich; as having nothing, and yet possessing all things . . . We have spoken openly to you, our heart is wide open.

*General response:*

_____

_____

_____

_____

*Personal response:*

_____

_____

_____

_____

❈

## DISCUSSION POINT

Is it more important to be right in an argument with another person, or to be at peace with that person? What does God desire? How difficult is it to turn away from feelings of vengeance?

_____

_____

_____

_____

## TALKING AND LISTENING UNTIL YOU REACH UNDERSTANDING

When two people are talking, and they are willing to keep on talking to each other and *listening* to each other, they are much more likely to come to a resolution. Real understanding is rarely achieved in cold silence!

Don't tell me that you love another person, but you are unwilling to talk to that person. Don't tell me that you love another person, but you just can't open up and be transparent about your feelings, ideas, or your past experiences. Don't tell me that you love another person, but you are unwilling to work on getting to the core issue of a problem that exists between you. Any time you say, "I love her, *but* . . ." or "I love him *when* . . . ," you have just told me that you don't really love that person or value that relationship.

On the other hand, if two people are willing to keep talking, keep discussing, keep open to each other, and keep listening, those two people have a real chance of reaching a mutually satisfying agreement and a peaceful resolution of their differences. That doesn't mean one person does all the talking and the other does the listening. A mutuality of talking and listening is required.

Two people with differences need to learn to seek *understanding*—which is more than mere information. They need to get to the heart of a disagreement, including motives, desires, and needs that may not have been spoken. They need to be honest about their own emotions and be clear in stating what they would like the nature of the relationship to be or become. (From *Finding Peace*, pages 167–168)

## REFLECTION AND RESPONSE

The Bible has numerous admonitions to us to "get understanding." Real understanding, which comes only by extensive talking and listening and great transparency and vulnerability in communication, is at the center of a peaceful, strong relationship. This kind of understanding is also a gift from God. Ask the Lord for it. In one of the passages below, Solomon asked God for wisdom as he began his reign as king of Israel. Take special note of God's response. Keep in mind that part of God's wisdom for you is wisdom in how to deal with other people and build loving, godly relationships with them. Reflect upon this passage and the other passages below, noting especially key words and phrases that the Holy Spirit seems to emphasize to your spirit. How important is understanding to the longevity and blessing of any relationship you seek to develop?

PROVERBS 2:1–9~My son, if you receive my words,
>And treasure my commands within you,
>So that you incline your ear to wisdom,
>And apply your heart to understanding;
>Yes, if you cry out for discernment,
>And lift up your voice for understanding,
>If you seek her as silver,
>And search for her as for hidden treasures;
>Then you will understand the fear of the LORD,
>And find the knowledge of God.
>For the LORD gives wisdom;
>From His mouth come knowledge and understanding;
>He stores up sound wisdom for the upright;
>He is a shield to those who walk uprightly;
>He guards the paths of justice,
>And preserves the way of His saints.

Then you will understand righteousness and justice,
Equity and every good path.

*General response:*

_____

_____

_____

_____

*Personal response:*

_____

_____

_____

_____

PROVERBS 11:12~He who is devoid of wisdom despises his neighbor,
But a man of understanding holds his peace.

*General response:*

_____

_____

_____

_____

*Personal response:*

_____

_____

_____

_____

# RESPONDING TO THOSE WHO ARE "ENEMIES"

What guidance does God give us as to how we should treat our enemies? We are called to trust God with our feelings of anger and vengeance. Paul is very specific:

> If your enemy is hungry, feed him;
> If he is thirsty, give him a drink. (Rom. 12:20)

God promises to reward those who treat their enemies well.

In Bible times, to give food and water to a hungry, thirsty enemy was a sign of tremendous hospitality. People knew that if you turned a hungry, thirsty enemy away from your tent out into the wilderness, that enemy would only seek to do you more harm. Showing basic kindness to the enemy, on the other hand, was a means of defusing their anger and possibly putting a stop to their evil actions.

What was true about enemies and persecution in Bible times holds true today! The only possibility of turning an enemy into a friend is by showing kindness to that person. Enemies don't become friends by force or by acts of vengeance. Rather, our enemies become friends when we express the love of God to them, do good to them, speak well of them, and pray for them. (From *Finding Peace*, pages 176–177)

### REFLECTION AND RESPONSE

A person who comes against you to harass you, demean you, or persecute you repeatedly takes on the identity of an enemy, especially if you are being harassed, demeaned, or persecuted for your relationship with Jesus Christ. How are we to deal with such people? Reflect upon the following verses and ask the Holy Spirit to reveal His wisdom to you.

MATTHEW 5:44~[Jesus taught:] "Love your enemies, bless those who curse you, do good to those who hate you, and pray for those who spitefully use you and persecute you."

*General response:*

_____

_____

_____

_____

_____

*Personal response:*

_____

_____

_____

_____

PROVERBS 24:17–18~Do not rejoice when your enemy falls,
> And do not let your heart be glad when he stumbles;
> Lest the LORD see it, and it displease Him,
> And He turn away His wrath from him.

*General response:*

_____

_____

_____

_____

*Personal response:*

_____

_____

_____

_____

# How Much Should You Compromise to Reach Peace?

The Bible gives a very clear answer. We are to compromise according to the strength, grace, goodness, and love God gives us, all the way to the point where compromising would mean violating a scriptural principle or commandment.

If your compromise means caving in to evil, breaking a commandment related to morality, denying or rebelling against a principle related to godly relationships, turning away from the Bible as the truth of God, or turning away from following Jesus as your Lord, then you must not compromise. You must not violate the Word of God.

Forgive a person seventy times seven? Yes.

Go the second mile, third mile, even the hundredth mile? Yes.

Disobey God's Word—either His commandments or basic principles? No.

Jesus could have achieved peace by compromising with the religious leaders of His day, but to do so would have been to violate the principles of God's love, forgiveness, and grace extended to "whosoever" might believe in His name and be saved. Jesus did not compromise for "peace at any price," and He does not call us to seek peace at any price.

When it comes to God's Word, the person who believes in relative truth, as compared to absolute truth, tends to say, "Well, that's what *you* believe. That's *your* interpretation."

I assure you of this: If you refuse to compromise your deeply held convictions, the call of God on your life, and the truth of God's Word, then God will stand with you. Furthermore, He will turn any persecution you experience to your eternal benefit. He will bring about spiritual growth, greater faith, and stronger enduring power in you. He will reward you either on earth or in heaven for your stand. And He will give you His peace! (From *Finding Peace*, pages 184, 186)

## Reflection and Response

The repeated admonition of the Lord is to stand firm in the faith. As you read, reflect upon, and respond to the following verses, note especially words or phrases that stand out to you. Ask the Lord what it is He desires for you to learn.

PROVERBS 12:7~The wicked are overthrown and are no more,
But the house of the righteous will stand.

*General response:*

_____

_____

_____

_____

*Personal response:*

_____

_____

_____

_____

2 CORINTHIANS 1:24~By faith you stand.

*General response:*

_____

_____

_____

_____

*Personal response:*

_____

_____

_____

_____

NEHEMIAH 9:5~Stand up and bless the LORD your God forever and ever!

*General response:*

_____

_____

_____

_____

*Personal response:*

_____

_____

_____

_____

※

## Thanks and Praise

Now is the time to praise the Lord for the many ways in which He has helped you to develop strong, godly relationships, to deal with your enemies in a godly manner, and to stand strong in the face of opposition and persecution. Identify at least ten attributes or experiences in which the Lord has been faithful to you in helping you develop and preserve loving relationships. You may find yourself listing the names of family members and friends with thanks and praise for these relationships!

_____

_____

_____

_____

_____

_____

_____

_____

_____

# TWELVE

# OVERCOMING FEAR

## THE OPPOSITE OF FEAR IS FAITH

Many people think the opposite of fear is hope, or courage, or strength. The true opposite of fear is *faith*. And when fear causes paralysis, it not only quenches one's peace but it attacks the foundation of that peace—namely, our faith. Peace goes out the window when fear is present.

Much of fear is rooted in doubt that God will be present, provide justice or help, or be capable of dealing with the crisis at hand. Faith says, "Yes, God is here. Yes, God will provide. Yes, God is capable of all things!"

Much of fear is rooted in threats—sometimes threatening words, sometimes threatening behavior. Faith says, "I will not be traumatized by threats. I will act wisely, not fearfully. I believe God will prevent the threat from ever coming to pass. And if the threat does comes to pass, I believe God will help me deal with whatever is thrown at me." (From *Finding Peace*, pages 187–188)

### REFLECTION AND RESPONSE

Recall the most frightening experience you believe you have ever faced. (The good news is that you faced it and lived through it!) Be specific:

Who was involved?

_____

_____

What happened, and where did this occur?

_____

_____

_____

How did you respond?

_____

_____

_____

Why do you believe you were gripped with fear? (What was the threat? What did you perceive to be the potential consequences?)

_____

_____

_____

As you look back over your statements above, what role did faith play in helping you overcome this fearful experience?

_____

_____

_____

As you read the verses below, note the importance God places on our having an active and strong faith to combat the fears of life. Our faith is rooted in truly knowing who God is, seeing God's hand in the course of our lives—past, present, and future—and catching a glimpse of all that God is capable of doing!

∞

*Reflect upon and then respond to the verses below in both* general *and* personal *ways. Indicate what you believe to be the general message of these passages, and then identify what you believe the Lord has as a personal message to you.*

2 TIMOTHY 1:7~For God has not given us a spirit of fear, but of power and of love and of a sound mind.

*General response:*

_____

_____

_____

_____

*Personal response:*

_____

_____

_____

_____

ISAIAH 44:6–8~Thus says the LORD the King of Israel,
    And his Redeemer, the LORD of hosts:
    "I am the First and I am the Last;
    Besides Me there is no God.
    And who can proclaim as I do?
    Then let him declare it and set it in order for Me,
    Since I appointed the ancient people.
    And the things that are coming and shall come,
    Let them show these to them.
    Do not fear, nor be afraid:
    Have I not told you from that time, and declared it?
    You are My witnesses.
    Is there a God besides Me?
    Indeed there is no other Rock;
    I know not one."

*General response:*

_____

_____

_____

_____

*Personal response:*

_____

_____

_____

_____

LUKE 12:32~[Jesus said:] "Do not fear, little flock, for it is your Father's good pleasure to give you the kingdom."

*General response:*

_____

_____

_____

_____

*Personal response:*

_____

_____

_____

_____

## DISCUSSION POINT

How important is it that we are able to see that God is with us, for us, and active on our behalf?

_____

_____

How important to our faith is our obedience in keeping the commandments of God's Word?

_____

_____

# IDENTIFY YOUR GREATEST FEARS

Identify your fears. What do you fear most? Death? Being alone? Old age? Do you fear being rejected, criticized, or losing someone you love? Do you fear poor health or perhaps the possibility of developing a particular disease? Do you fear a tragedy involving a child or spouse?

Fear can sometimes lurk in our hearts in such a subtle way that we don't even identify the feeling we have as fear. It may be that we have a sense of foreboding, an uneasiness, or a feeling of dread.

Let's take a look at several of the biggest and most common fears we all face.

## 1. FEAR OF SIN'S CONSEQUENCES

Fear is a normal and universal response to our knowing we have sinned and become separated from God. A recognition of our own sin always makes us feel exposed and vulnerable to God's judgment.

## 2. FEAR OF DANGER AND HARM

We have a number of natural, normal fears—such as the fear of falling, the fear associated with coming in contact with a burning stove, or the fear of crossing a busy freeway at rush hour. These are fears that help protect us and preserve life. They turn us away from harm and pain and help us avoid injury, not only physically but emotionally and spiritually.

## 3. FEAR OF EVIL

Spiritual dangers are just as real as physical dangers. It is *good* for a person to be fearful in evil situations, because that fear can and should drive you to pray, to trust God to deliver you from the power of evil, and to get as far away from evil as possible!

## 4. FEAR OF DISOBEYING GOD

It is also good to have a fear of disobeying God. That fear can and *should* compel a person to obey! (From *Finding Peace*, pages 190–194)

## A Letter to God

Take this opportunity to express your fears to the Lord. If you have found yourself identifying with any of the four specific fears above—fear of sin's consequences, fear of danger and harm, fear of evil, or fear of disobeying God—admit those fears to the Lord. Express to the Lord why you are afraid, to the extent that you know why. Ask the Lord to reveal to you any experience in your childhood that may have evoked these fears so you can invite the Lord to heal that experience fully. Express both natural fears and spiritual fears.

## What About a Fear of the Lord?

When we read in the Bible about having a "fear" of the Lord, that term *fear* actually refers to great reverence, honor, or awe. It is an awe rooted in our awareness that God governs all things and is absolutely righteous in all His judgments. An awesome awareness and reverence of the glory of God produce humility and obedience.

God also never intended that we live in fear that keeps us from seeking a deeper relationship with Him or that keeps us from going about normal daily life or fulfilling the responsibilities we have to others. Any fear that keeps you from being a witness for the gospel, makes you cower in weakness before other people, keeps you from reaching out in love to those in need, or keeps you from behaving in a rational manner is not a normal fear God intends for you to have! (From *Finding Peace*, page 193)

### Reflection and Response

It is very important that you understand we are not to be *afraid* of God. He is our loving, merciful, forgiving heavenly Father. The following verses are about the fear of the Lord. Note how they point toward the majesty and awesome power of God. Our response is to be one of reverence, honor, and awe—not fear. The end result is to be our obedience in following the Lord and trusting Him in all things.

DEUTERONOMY 10:12–21~[Moses said:] "And now, Israel, what does the LORD your God require of you, but to fear the LORD your God, to walk in all His ways and to love Him, to serve the LORD your God with all your heart and with all your soul, and to keep the commandments of the LORD and His statutes which I command you today for your good? Indeed heaven and the highest heavens belong to the LORD your God, also the earth with all that is in it. The LORD delighted only in your fathers, to love them; and He chose their descendants after them, you above all peoples, as it is this day. Therefore circumcise the foreskin of your heart, and be stiff-necked no longer. For the LORD your God is God of gods and Lord of lords, the great God, mighty and awesome, who shows no partiality nor takes a bribe. He administers justice for the fatherless and the widow, and loves the stranger, giving him food and clothing. Therefore love the stranger, for you were strangers in the land of Egypt. You shall fear the LORD your God, you shall serve Him, and to Him you shall hold fast, and take oaths in His name. He is your praise, and He is your God, who has done for you these great and awesome things which your eyes have seen."

*General response:*

_____

_____

_____

_____

*Personal response:*

_____

_____

_____

_____

## REAL OR SHADOW FEARS?

Shadow fears are not real. They reside only in our imaginations or our minds. If they persist or grow, they can result in a person's developing a "spirit of fear."

A spirit of fear enslaves a person's mind and heart. The person who has a spirit of fear, which may be anything from a serious phobia to a paralyzing or crippling fear that keeps that person from functioning normally in relationships with other people, is a person who becomes a *slave* to fear. Such a person won't go certain places, engage in certain activities, or speak out in certain situations because he or she fears great loss, injury, persecution, or retribution.

The first goal many of us have when dealing with fear is determining if the fear we feel is legitimate or if it is a shadow fear.

The key questions we must ask in determining whether a fear is normal, real, and helpful or if it is debilitating, enslaving, and paralyzing are these: "What does God say about this fear? Does He say that this is something I should fear? Or does He say that He is sufficient in all ways to meet my needs so that I don't need to fear this thing, this relationship, this action, this possibility, or this situation?" (From *Finding Peace*, pages 196–198)

### REFLECTION AND RESPONSE

The verses below are related to instances in the Bible that give us insight into what we *should* fear and *should not* fear. Relate these admonitions of God's Word to your career, your family, your community, or your church. Ask the Holy Spirit to reveal to you what He is trying to teach you in these passages.

MATTHEW 10:28–31~[Jesus said:] "Do not fear those who kill the body but cannot kill the soul. But rather fear Him who is able to destroy both soul and body in hell. Are not two sparrows sold for a copper coin? And not one of them falls to the ground apart from your Father's will. But the very hairs of your head are all numbered. Do not fear therefore; you are of more value than many sparrows."

*General response:*

_____

_____

_____

_____

*Personal response:*

_____

_____

_____

_____

PSALM 49:16–17~Do not be afraid when one becomes rich,
> When the glory of his house is increased;
> For when he dies he shall carry nothing away;
> His glory shall not descend after him.

*General response:*

_____

_____

_____

_____

*Personal response:*

_____

_____

_____

_____

JEREMIAH 1:7–8~But the LORD said to me:

> "Do not say, 'I am a youth,'
> For you shall go to all to whom I send you,
> And whatever I command you, you shall speak.
> Do not be afraid of their faces,
> For I am with you to deliver you," says the LORD.

*General response:*

_____

_____

_____

_____

*Personal response:*

_____

_____

_____

_____

1 PETER 3:14–16~Even if you should suffer for righteousness' sake, you are blessed. "And do not be afraid of their threats, nor be troubled." But sanctify the Lord God in your hearts, and always be ready to give a defense to everyone who asks you a reason for the hope that is in you, with meekness and fear; having a good conscience, that when they defame you as evildoers, those who revile your good conduct in Christ may be ashamed.

*General response:*

_____

_____

_____

_____

NOTE: In this brief passage, we find both the fear of man and what man can do, and the fear of God. How different are these fears! (Remember that "fear of the Lord" refers more to reverence and awe at God's infinite power to act, *not* that God is threatening to do harm to a person or group.)

*Personal response:*

_____

_____

_____

_____

## SEVEN STEPS TO OVERCOMING FEAR

There are several steps we can take to overcome fear.

### 1. ACKNOWLEDGE THE FEAR YOU EXPERIENCE

Acknowledge that you are fearful. Ask God to help you identify the fear—to name it, define it, and bring it to the surface of your conscience so you can talk about it and confess its presence to the Lord.

Don't just accept a fear in your life as something harmless. The reality is that fear keeps you from going some places God desires you to go. It can keep you from doing some things that God may desire you to do.

## 2. ASK IMMEDIATELY FOR GOD'S HELP

Go to your heavenly Father immediately to ask Him to help you conquer your fear. Ask the Lord to cleanse your mind of fearful thoughts. Ask Him to protect your mind from gripping fear. Ask Him to prepare you to counteract fear in positive, strong ways.

## 3. DETERMINE THE ROOT FEAR

Ask God to help you identify any emotions that may be linked to fear, such as:

> Greed—fear of not having enough
>
> Rejection—fear of not being accepted
>
> Guilt—fear of being found out
>
> Lack of confidence—fear of failure
>
> Anger—fear of not getting your own way, losing control or esteem
>
> Jealousy—fear of not having what you believe is rightfully yours
>
> Indecisiveness—fear of criticism, fear of making a wrong decision

## 4. GO TO GOD'S WORD

Read and memorize verses that deal with fear. Focus on passages in which various individuals in the Bible faced fear.

## 5. PRAISE THE LORD

As you read and speak God's Word, accompany the truth of God's Word with your vocal and frequent praise.

## 6. TAKE A POSITIVE STEP

I believe it is very important for a person to confront fear by taking a positive step in faith. Do something that gives you an experience in which God can reveal to you that He is greater than the fear you have felt.

## 7. MAKE A DECISION

Come to a firm decision that you are not going to live in fear. Make a choice to believe God—yes, believe Him more than you believe your own emotions. Make a decision that you are going to believe in God, who loves you, provides for you, cares for you, is always available to you, and is in control of your life at all times. Make a decision to trust Him. (From *Finding Peace*, pages 198–208)

## REFLECTION AND RESPONSE

Below are several passages that call us to admit our fear to the Lord or to trust Him to be our ever-present help in times of fear. Note specific words or phrases that seem to stand out to you in a special way.

PSALM 55:4–7~My heart is severely pained within me,
And the terrors of death have fallen upon me.
Fearfulness and trembling have come upon me,
And horror has overwhelmed me.
So I said, "Oh, that I had wings like a dove!
I would fly away and be at rest.
Indeed, I would wander far off,
And remain in the wilderness."

*General response:*

_____

_____

_____

_____

*Personal response:*

_____

_____

_____

_____

PSALM 34:4~I sought the LORD, and He heard me,
And delivered me from all my fears.

*General response:*

_____

_____

_____

_____

*Personal response:*

_____

_____

_____

_____

PSALM 56~Be merciful to me, O God, for man would swallow me up;
Fighting all day he oppresses me.
My enemies would hound me all day,
For there are many who fight against me, O Most High.
Whenever I am afraid,
I will trust in You.
In God (I will praise His word),
In God I have put my trust;
I will not fear.
What can flesh do to me?
All day they twist my words;
All their thoughts are against me for evil.
They gather together,
They hide, they mark my steps,
When they lie in wait for my life.

Shall they escape by iniquity?

In anger cast down the peoples, O God!

You number my wanderings;

Put my tears into Your bottle;

Are they not in Your book?

When I cry out to You,

Then my enemies will turn back;

This I know, because God is for me.

In God (I will praise His word),

In the LORD (I will praise His word),

In God I have put my trust;

I will not be afraid.

What can man do to me?

Vows made to You are binding upon me, O God;

I will render praises to You,

For You have delivered my soul from death.

Have You not kept my feet from falling,

That I may walk before God

In the light of the living?


*General response:*

_____

_____

_____

_____


*Personal response:*

_____

_____

_____

_____

## A Letter to God

As you have read through the statement from *Finding Peace* and the several related Bible passages, have you felt an urgency about any step you need to take in overcoming fear? Have you identified the deep fear that seems to exist under the surface fear? Take this opportunity to write a letter to God, being very honest with Him and with yourself about where you are in taking the necessary steps to overcoming your fear. Express to the Lord your desire to take the next step as He reveals it to you.

## THIRTEEN

∞

# LEARNING TO LIVE IN CONTENTMENT

One of the greatest lessons that you can learn as you learn to live in contentment is this: You have the power to *respond* to any situation, not merely react to it. The power of the Holy Spirit resident in you will always enable you to confront a problem with faith and wisdom if you will only trust Him. (From *Finding Peace*, page 215)

### REFLECTION AND RESPONSE

In *Finding Peace*, I noted that the apostle Paul faced both external struggles and internal struggles. He listed the external struggles to the church at Corinth—he was beaten with rods, stoned, lashed with a whip, shipwrecked, in peril of robbers and in danger as he traveled, frequently imprisoned, threatened frequently with death, and knew what it meant to be hungry, thirsty, cold, without sufficient clothing, and sleepless. He also knew what it meant to be criticized, falsely accused, misquoted, misunderstood, and rejected. (See 2 Corinthians 11:23–29.) Paul also wrote that he faced an internal struggle—namely, that he sometimes did those things he wanted to avoid doing, and sometimes didn't do what he wanted to do. He wrote about a "thorn in the flesh" that was a point of discouragement to him. And yet, from *prison*, Paul wrote the Philippians about "contentment" and in his letter, he used the phrase "joy of the Lord" sixteen times.

As you read the following verses, ask the Lord to reveal to you what He desires to teach you about contentment.

∞

*Reflect upon and then respond to the verses below in both* general *and* personal *ways. Indicate what you believe to be the* general *message of these passages, and then identify what you believe the Lord has as a* personal *message to you.*

PHILIPPIANS 4:11–13~I have learned in whatever state I am, to be content: I know how to be abased, and I know how to abound. Everywhere and in all things I have learned both to be full and to be hungry, both to abound and to suffer need. I can do all things through Christ who strengthens me.

*General response:*

_____

_____

_____

_____

*Personal response:*

_____

_____

_____

_____

1 PETER 5:6–7~Humble yourselves under the mighty hand of God, that He may exalt you in due time, casting all your care upon Him, for He cares for you.

*General response:*

_____

_____

_____

_____

*Personal response:*

_____

_____

_____

_____

_____

1 TIMOTHY 6:6–10~Now godliness with contentment is great gain. For we brought nothing into this world, and it is certain we can carry nothing out. And having food and clothing, with these we shall be content. But those who desire to be rich fall into temptation and a snare, and into many foolish and harmful lusts which drown men in destruction and perdition. For the love of money is a root of all kinds of evil, for which some have strayed from the faith in their greediness, and pierced themselves through with many sorrows.

*General response:*

_____

_____

_____

_____

*Personal response:*

_____

_____

_____

_____

∞

## DISCUSSION POINT

The world tells us that if we just have enough money or material resources, we will enjoy security and contentment. God's Word says something quite different! How difficult is it in this generation to live without greed or a love of money—to be content with just having sufficient food and clothing?

_____

_____

_____

_____

## Four Keys to Living in Contentment

To live in a lasting, confident state of inner contentment, there are several things you must do:

### 1. CUT THE CONDITIONAL BONDS

Recognize that there is nothing you can do to make another person love you unconditionally. They either do or they don't. There's no earning unconditional love. There's no amount of striving that wins unconditional love. There are no formulas or prescriptions that ensure the unconditional love of another person. In fact, the very words *earn* and *strive* are ones that apply if love is *conditional!*

*Turn to God for unconditional love.* Ask the Lord to help you experience His love in a new way. Be still before the Lord. Open your heart to Him. Ask Him to speak to you and to let you feel His close presence.

*Seek friends who love unconditionally.* Another thing we can do when we are caught up in the vise of trying to earn conditional love is to seek out people who know how to love unconditionally. I'm not at all encouraging a spouse to turn to a person of the opposite sex for love, affection, or a sexual relationship. But rather, I am encouraging deep, abiding, and godly friendships with mentors and peers of the same sex who can provide unconditional love.

### 2. CAST ALL YOUR CARES ON THE LORD

Beyond receiving the unconditional love of God and others, to live in abiding contentment you must continually cast *all* your cares on the Lord.

### 3. STAY IN THE WORD

In going through difficult times in my life, one of the great blessings of God to me has been the fact that as a pastor I've had the responsibility for preaching regularly, and that, in turn, has required me to stay in the Word. There's no substitute for being in the Word daily—reading it as nourishment for your soul just as regularly as you take in food for your body. Your Bible is the number one way God speaks to you in a daily way. It is His message to you—His directives, His opinions, His advice, His words of love and comfort, His faith-building admonitions, and His commands. Trust me on this—the Lord has a way of speaking to you as you read and meditate on the Scriptures so that you will know it is the Lord who is speaking.

## 4. TAKE CHARGE OF YOUR THINKING

You can control what you think. You and you alone have the ability and the responsibility for choosing what you will focus your thoughts upon.

So many people just react to what is happening around them. Reactions usually begin in our emotions, and the result is that our thoughts become bound up in our emotions, most of which are negative emotions of fear and doubt in a time of severe crisis. Other people react to highly negative circumstances by becoming paralyzed by confusion, tension, and inner turmoil. None of these reactions are what God desires for us!

God calls us to *respond* to life, not merely react to it. Certainly we may react in the initial first moment or two of a negative circumstance or crisis. But very quickly, we must speak to our mind, *Don't panic. God is in control! Believe! Trust!* (From *Finding Peace*, pages 215–225)

### REFLECTION AND RESPONSE

One of the people in the Bible who encountered a very stressful situation—one that easily could have robbed her of inner peace and sent her into a tailspin of anxiety—was Mary, the mother of Jesus, at the time she first learned she was pregnant. As you read through Mary's response to Elizabeth, who had greeted her with a tremendous blessing, note how Mary did the four things I have stated above: She received God's unconditional love, cast her cares on the Lord, remembered His Word, and took charge of her thinking. As you reflect upon this passage of Scripture below, ask the Holy Spirit to show you what He desires for you to learn. Note any words or concepts that seem to stand out to you in a special way.

LUKE 1:46–56~And Mary said:

> "My soul magnifies the Lord,
> And my spirit has rejoiced in God my Savior.

For He has regarded the lowly state of His maidservant;
For behold, henceforth all generations will call me blessed.
For He who is mighty has done great things for me,
And holy is His name.
And His mercy is on those who fear Him
From generation to generation.
He has shown strength with His arm;
He has scattered the proud in the imagination of their hearts.
He has put down the mighty from their thrones,
And exalted the lowly.
He has filled the hungry with good things,
And the rich He has sent away empty.
He has helped His servant Israel,
In remembrance of His mercy,
As He spoke to our fathers,
To Abraham and to his seed forever."

And Mary remained with her [Elizabeth] about three months, and returned to her house.

*General response:*

_____

_____

_____

_____

*Personal response:*

_____

_____

_____

_____

## A Letter to God

Now is the time to tell the Lord the struggles you have with living in contentment. Tell the Lord how difficult it is for you to give or to receive unconditional love—explore the reasons why this may be true. Tell the Lord about your struggles to cast all your care on Him, on your struggle to stay in the Word—reading it daily, memorizing it, and reciting it to your own ears. Tell the Lord about any struggles you have in controlling your own thoughts. Ask the Lord for His help.

## MAINTAIN YOUR FOCUS ON THE LORD

To live in inner contentment, the entire focus of your life must be the Lord Jesus Christ.

I've had short periods in my life when a particular problem or situation would cause me to have nights in which I'd toss and turn hour after hour, unable to sleep. I have discovered that the best thing I can do when I can't seem to let go of thinking about a particular problem, conversation, or criticism, is to get out of bed, get down on my knees, and cry out to God, "Please help me through this. Help me to focus on You and You alone."

Sleep comes when my focus is on the Lord and on how He would have me think or respond in my emotions to a particular situation. Sleep is elusive when I allow my focus to get on what others have said, all the things that might happen, or the difficulty of a challenge that lies ahead. The choice is really very simple—think about the Lord and His abundant provision, protection, and love, or think about all the people and circumstances that are trying to rob you of provision, destroy your life, or heap hatred upon you.

Thinking about the Lord brings a person peace. Thinking about anything else is usually a shortcut to anxiety, fear, or worry. (From *Finding Peace*, pages 226–227)

### REFLECTION AND RESPONSE

There are a number of verses in the Bible that refer to our great need for maintaining a focus on the Lord and that refer to the great blessing that comes when we do. One of the most powerful stories about this in the Old Testament involves Moses and a battle the Israelites fought against the Amalekites. The raised rod of Moses in the following passage was a strong sign to all of the Israelites fighting in the valley below that God was present with them. It was a sign that helped them put their focus on God.

EXODUS 17:8–13~Now Amalek came and fought with Israel in Rephidim. And Moses said to Joshua, "Choose us some men and go out, fight with Amalek. Tomorrow I will stand on the top of the hill with the rod of God in my hand." So Joshua did as Moses said to him, and fought with Amalek. And Moses, Aaron, and Hur went up to the top of the hill. And so it was when Moses held up his hand, that Israel prevailed; and when he let down his hand, Amalek prevailed. But Moses' hands became heavy; so they took a stone and put it under him, and he sat on it. And Aaron and Hur supported his hands, one on one side, and the other on the other side; and his hands were steady until the going down of the sun. So Joshua defeated Amalek and his people with the edge of the sword.

*General response:*

_____

_____

_____

_____

*Personal response:*

_____

_____

_____

_____

PSALM 63:1–8 ~ O GOD, You are my God;
   Early will I seek You;
   My soul thirsts for You;
   My flesh longs for You
   In a dry and thirsty land
   Where there is no water.
   So I have looked for You in the sanctuary,
   To see Your power and Your glory.
   Because Your lovingkindness is better than life,
   My lips shall praise You.
   Thus I will bless You while I live;
   I will lift up my hands in Your name.
   My soul shall be satisfied as with marrow and fatness,
   And my mouth shall praise You with joyful lips.
   When I remember You on my bed,

I meditate on You in the night watches.

Because You have been my help,

Therefore in the shadow of Your wings I will rejoice.

My soul follows close behind You;

Your right hand upholds me.

*General response:*

_____

_____

_____

_____

_____

*Personal response:*

_____

_____

_____

_____

_____

∞

## DISCUSSION POINT

How difficult is it to turn your eyes away from a problem—especially an abiding problem—and put your focus on the Lord? What helps you most in doing this?

_____

_____

_____

_____

_____

_____

## A Grievance Statement

Is there someone who has loved you *conditionally* in the past or present? Have you ever faced up to the fact that conditional love can create an abiding state of anxiety in your life? Is there a problem that seems to control your thought life—it may be an obsession, an addiction, or a deep desire? Is this problem associated with a particular person? Is there someone who continually criticizes you for trusting in God or belittles you for the time you spend in the Word of God? Take this opportunity to write a grievance statement to the Lord about this!

Were you raised by a parent, or perhaps influenced by some other authority figure in your early years, who did not live in contentment, and who passed on to you a prevailing lack of contentment? Again, take this opportunity to address that situation.

Have you ever faced up to the fact that there are godly things—godly goals, the pursuit of godly desires, and godly relationships—that the devil will do his utmost to *keep* you from thinking about? Rather, he fills your mind with memories and lusts (for people, possessions, prestige, and power) to keep you continually agitated. Take on the devil in your grievance statement.

Tell the Lord about specific incidents, the depth of feeling and anxiety you feel, or the "blame" you are placing on another person for your lack of contentment.

You may write your grievance statement below or on another sheet of paper.

_____

_____

_____

_____

_____

_____
_____
_____
_____
_____
_____
_____
_____
_____
_____
_____
_____
_____
_____
_____
_____
_____
_____
_____
_____
_____

After you have thoroughly expressed to the Lord all that you feel, ask the Lord to take your deep anxieties and to replace them with His peace.

## LIVING A CHRIST-CENTERED LIFE

A self-centered person is a person who thinks, *My needs, my desires, my wants, and my ideas must be met, enacted, and fulfilled.* Such a person tends to talk nonstop about "my career, my accomplishments, my awards, my car, my house, my clothes, my vacation, my pleasure, my, my, my, my." Such a person nearly always is very insensitive to others and a manipulator of people and situations.

The opposite of being self-centered is to be Christ-centered. It is to say, "What Christ wants is what I want. What pleases Christ is what I desire."

Show me a person who is overflowing in generous friendship to another person, and I'll show you a person rich in friendships.

Show me a person who is extremely generous in the giving of her time to other people, and I'll show you a person who always has people "there" for her in times of her need.

Show me a person who can't give enough of himself to further the specific ministry calling that God has placed on his life, and I'll show you a person who has a tremendous sense of purpose and fulfillment.

The person who does not give is a person who does not receive. Such a person cannot experience peace.

Friend, Jesus is the source of your contentment. When you by faith enter into a personal relationship with Jesus, you will experience peace. (From *Finding Peace*, pages 228–230)

### REFLECTION AND RESPONSE

A Christ-centered person will want to do what Jesus would do. He or she will want to do all that Jesus commands. He will be a giver to others, not only spiritually, but materially and emotionally. As you read through and reflect upon the following verses, ask the Lord to help you become a Christ-centered person rather than a self-centered person.

MATTHEW 26:39~He [Jesus] went a little farther and fell on His face, and prayed, saying, "O My Father, if it is possible, let this cup pass from Me; nevertheless, not as I will, but as You will."

*General response:*

_____

_____

_____

_____

*Personal response:*

_____

_____

_____

_____

PHILIPPIANS 1:12, 19–21~But I want you to know, brethren, that the things which happened to me have actually turned out for the furtherance of the gospel . . . For I know that this will turn out for my deliverance through your prayer and the supply of the Spirit of Jesus Christ, according to my earnest expectation and hope that in nothing I shall be ashamed, but with all boldness, as always, so now also Christ will be magnified in my body, whether by life or by death. For to me, to live is Christ, and to die is gain.

*General response:*

_____

_____

_____

*Personal response:*

_____

_____

_____

_____

### THANKS AND PRAISE

Take this opportunity to praise God for all that He has done, is doing, and has promised to do to direct you in the paths of peace and to live in a state of genuine contentment. I encourage you to make a list of at least ten things that evoke in you feelings of deep peace and contentment. Include things both material and spiritual, practical and specific, as well as emotional and general. See God as the Creator of these things. As His Word says, "Every good gift and every perfect gift is from above, and comes down from the Father of lights, with whom there is no variation or shadow of turning" (James 1:17).

_____

_____

_____

_____

_____

_____

_____

_____

_____

_____

# APPENDIX

In the beginning of this workbook you found brief directions on how to get the most out of your study. And you also found directions to go to the end of the workbook for expanded information on how to go even deeper in the material—this is the tool you may use to do just that. I hope you find it helpful.

This workbook is intended to accompany the book titled *Finding Peace* (Thomas Nelson Publishers 2003). You will see references to *Finding Peace* from time to time, along with the page numbers from that book which I have referenced in this workbook.

There are four features that are repeated frequently in this workbook.

## KEY FEATURE 1:
## REFLECT AND RESPOND

One of the great ways of studying God's Word is to sit and read a passage of God's Word, and then pause to reflect upon what that passage really says. This is the most basic form of Bible "study." As you read the Bible, simply take a look at certain key words or phrases that might pop out at you in a special way. Think about why God is saying what He is saying—what are the consequences associated with what He says, what are the benefits to a person who does what He says, what are the guidelines related to human behavior and relationships, and what does the passage say about the great mission of getting the gospel of Jesus Christ to the whole world?

Perhaps the most important question you can ask about a passage in the Bible is this: "How does this relate to *me?*" The Bible is not only applicable to all people of all ages in all cultures and races at all times in history. It is also God's personal word to *you*—right now, right where you are, right in the middle of the circumstances in which you find yourself.

Please note that asking "How does this relate to me?" is not the same as asking "What does this say to me?" or "What does this mean to me?" Those who approach the Bible with a

"What does this say to me?" attitude very often are looking for ways in which the Bible jus-tifies or supports their particular man-made point of view. They are seeking ways in which the Bible upholds what they already choose to believe and think, rather than looking to the Bible as the authoritative Word of God and trusting the Bible to speak to their lives in order to mold and transform what they believe and think. The two approaches are 180 degrees apart. The Bible is not subject to individual interpretation. The Bible, however, is applicable to every individual in very specific ways at specific times. The question "How does this relate to me?" should be asked with an honest and open mind and heart—it is a question that invites the Holy Spirit to reply, "*This* is what I'm trying to say to *you* right now in your life—*This* is how My commandments, promises, and words of comfort are meant to be applied to your situation, decisions, and needs."

## FAITH AND ACTION

Reflection isn't enough, however. God's Word always compels us to take action. God calls us to *respond* to what He says in His Word. Our first response is a response of *faith*—"I *believe* that what God says in His Word is true for all people. I *believe* this is true for me. I have faith to *believe* that God is always true to His Word and His promises—what He has said and done for others, He is saying and will do for me."

Our second response is a response of *action*. God's Word is not only for the "believing" but for the "doing." James 1:22 tells us clearly, "Be doers of the word, and not hearers only." That passage goes on to say that if we only hear the Word and do nothing about it, we are like a person who looks in a mirror and sees himself and then walks away and promptly for-gets what he saw. It is not the forgetful hearer who is blessed and who grows to maturity in Christ Jesus. Rather, it is the one who believes God's Word and lives it out—obeying God's commandments, doing what God says to do, and reaching out to others as God compels him or her to share the gospel.

Now what does that have to do with this workbook?

Two things.

First, as part of the *Reflection and Response* sections, you are going to be asked to respond to verses from the Bible that relate to a particular topic. You will see the words *General response* and *Personal response*.

The phrase *General response* is my challenge to you to find the key concept in the verse or passage—the central meaning that applies to all people, all the time.

The phrase *Personal response* is my challenge to you to state what you believe God is saying to you very personally. God's personal word to you is very directional and concrete—it is the applying of the verse to people, places, things, and situations you are facing.

When people study journalism they usually learn the "5 W's and H" approach to reporting. Every good journalist is taught to ask: Who? What? When? Where? Why? How?

These questions also can be used in a personal application of God's Word. Let me give you an example, using a verse that has little to do with finding peace—but has a great deal to do with this workbook.

Obey those who rule over you, and be submissive, for they watch out for your souls, as those who must give account. (Heb. 13:17)

## REFLECTION

I hope that as you reflect on this verse, you note the word *obey* and you reflect on what that word means. Then take a look at the phrase "rule over you." To rule over is to "have authority over or influence over." What kinds of authority do we each face in our lives? (Consider the differences between spiritual authority and political, civil, or legal authority.) Who has influence over you? What does it mean in a very practical way to "be submissive"? You could probably reflect on all three of those concepts for a very long time!

Now, from time to time a person puts himself under the "spiritual influence" of different people. Any time you watch a television program or listen to a radio program to hear a pastor preach the Word of God, you are putting yourself under the spiritual influence of that person. Any time you read a book by a Christian author, and the book is about the Bible or a spiritual practice such as prayer or stewardship, you are putting yourself under the spiritual influence of that person.

To a great extent, when you hear or read what a Christian leader has to say, you face a decision—are you going to *obey* what this person tells you to do? Are you going to open your mind and submit your thinking to what they preach from God's Word? Are you submitting your will before God so you can be taught? Or do you listen with your arms folded and your mind closed like a steel trap, virtually daring the preacher to try to get through to you? Do you do the same thing to the Holy Spirit who tries to instruct you day by day and hour by hour?

Oh, there's so much you can reflect on in just that one verse! And as you begin to work through this book in your hand, the following questions are very applicable: "Are you will-ing to be taught and to learn? Are you open to obeying what God's Word says and to sub-mitting to what the Holy Spirit speaks to your heart? Are you willing to allow me as a pastor to influence you and to teach you what I know about God's ways for finding peace?"

The truth is, if you aren't open to change, if you aren't open to learning from God's Word, if you aren't willing to submit yourself to the Holy Spirit, if you aren't willing to take in and meditate upon and apply what is said to you in this workbook or in the *Finding Peace* book . . . there is very little I can do to help you find peace in your personal life!

Take a look at the phrase "they watch out for your souls." That puts this entire sentence into a whole new light, doesn't it? This verse clearly refers to obedience and submission to those who are in spiritual authority over our lives—it has nothing to do with political, civil, or legal authority. I would hope that you would reflect upon who has spiritual authority over your life. Whose voice or voices are you listening to? Stop to consider for a moment what you are hearing, watching, or reading. Where are you going to church? What are you hear-ing and learning there?

I would hope that in reflecting upon this statement, you would also reflect upon the state of those who do not believe in Christ Jesus and who are not in a church fellowship and who do not have someone speaking the truth to them from God's Word. How vulnerable are they to the devil's attack since they aren't under the authority of anyone who "watches out for their souls"? How important is it to have people who will speak God's truth to our hearts in an ongoing way—day by day, week by week?

And the next phrase gives us an important insight into those to whom we must submit: "for they watch out for your souls, as those who must give account." Just because a person says that he or she has spiritual authority over you doesn't mean that the person actually *does* or *should*. Does the person who claims spiritual authority over you really care what happens to your eternal soul? Does the person teach you how to receive the gift of eternal life and how to be assured of your eternal salvation? Does the person teach you how to protect your soul against the devil's temptations, or how to receive all the spiritual blessings that God has for you? Do you sense spiritual humility in this person who claims authority over you—do you sense this person truly believes he or she must give account to God for the way you are taught and treated? These are just a few of the questions that are worthy of reflection. Ultimately, of course, the Holy Spirit has spiritual authority over your life and the life of every believer. How important is it for you to obey all that the Holy Spirit speaks to your heart and to do all that He tells you to do? Again, you could reflect for hours on that one question alone!

## RESPONSE

Your first response to the verse given above is a *faith response*. Do you really believe Hebrews 13:17? Do you believe it is God's word not only for two thousand years ago but for right now? Do you believe it is true for all believers around the world, yesterday, today, and forever?

Your second response is an *action response*. What do you believe this verse calls a person to do?

At the general level, what does this verse call all people to do? What would be the result in the church if all believers did this?

At the personal level, what is this verse saying to *you*?

*Who?* To whom are you to submit? To whom are you to look for teaching and inspiration—for insights into God's Word, for wisdom? Which voices and books are you to seek out so you might grow in the Lord?

*What?* What are you to obey? Ultimately, we are to obey the Word of God. Does what a person teaches you line up with the Word of God?

*When?* Is there a particular incident, time, or situation in which God seems to be asking you to submit yourself right now? Is there a particular lesson God seems especially trying to teach you right now? Is He leading you to study the Bible on a particular subject or to learn more about a particular biblical principle? Is He leading you to take a particular course or read a particular book?

*Where?* Are you fully comfortable submitting to the spiritual authority that is presently over you? Do you trust that person to "watch out for your soul"? Do you sense that the person feels a responsibility to give account to God for what you are taught and how you are treated? Are you where you should be? If not, where should you go? Under whose authority should you place yourself?

Another way to ask these questions: Are you involved in the church where you should be involved? Are you listening to what you should be listening to? Are you reading and studying what you should be reading and studying?

*Why?* List all the pros and cons of why it is important to you personally to be under good spiritual influence, to obey what is taught you, and to take action on what a spiritual leader challenges you to do.

*How?* How might you act on this verse right now? What steps need to be taken?

"That's a lot of work for just one verse!" you might be saying.

You're right!

I have shared all this in great detail for a reason. Study on any subject can be as superficial or as deep as you choose to make it. As you study any subject—including the subject of finding peace—you can look at that subject from many angles. You will only gain from any workbook what you are willing to put into that workbook in terms of time, effort, and depth of your personal reflection, application, and response. You might skim through this workbook in just a few hours. On the other hand . . . you might find yourself working on the concepts in this workbook for several months.

I encourage you to allow the truth of God's Word to sink deep into your soul. Let it nourish you, build you up, change you, and mold you into the person God wants you to be. Nobody finds all the peace they will ever need in an hour or a day. We only find the Source of all peace quickly—His name is Jesus. It is as we develop a lifetime relationship with Him that He leads us into the personal disciplines and the depth of faith that truly give us ongoing peace.

## TO SHARE OR NOT TO SHARE

Not everything that you reflect about, and certainly not all of your responses, should necessarily be made public.

This workbook can certainly be used for group discussions or a small-group Bible study. In fact, I encourage you to get involved in group Bible study and to talk over some of the concepts of this book with other people. There's great benefit in hearing the experiences and insights of other people.

But *all* that you write in *Reflection and Response* need not be shared. Those things that are part of your *Personal response* in many cases should be kept private. Otherwise, you simply won't be as honest and your responses won't be complete.

We all know that at times when we were in school we wrote down answers to test questions or said things in essays because we thought what we were writing was what the teacher wanted to read. We were looking for the approval of another person, rather than looking at the answer as a means of understanding our own selves or the subject matter.

That can easily happen when the "answers" to a workbook's questions are subjected to a small-group discussion. You may very well find yourself writing down things to say in the group discussion that you believe are things others in the group *want* to hear. You are likely to write down some responses because you think the group thinks those are the "right" or "most godly" responses to have. The result is that you may not be writing down what you really think or believe.

This workbook needs to reflect an honest statement to yourself about yourself. Because of that, I strongly recommend the following:

- Keep your workbook to yourself—refrain from looking at someone else's workbook. Don't allow others to read what you write.

- If you and other members of your family are involved in the same small-group discussion, have a separate workbook for each person.

- Keep your workbook in a place where it will remain private. Don't stick it in a drawer at work where a coworker may find it. Don't put it in a place where your children or spouse is likely to pick it up and thumb through it. Let your family members know that what you write in the workbook is similar to a diary. It's personal. It's private. Let it be known that you expect others to respect your privacy just as you respect what they write in their personal, private diaries.

You might also share this truth with your family members: What a person writes in a diary, journal, or workbook very often involves feelings or what a friend of mine calls "half-baked ideas." Feelings are fickle. What you feel one day may not be what you feel the next. The hurt you feel at one time may not be an abiding hurt—or it may be a hurt that God has healed or is healing! In other words, your statements about feelings should not be taken as absolute, set-in-concrete statements, either by you or anybody who might invade your privacy.

The same goes for opinions. Opinions grow, develop, and change as new information or new insights are gained, or as old memories may be recalled.

Does this mean that everything you write down in this workbook becomes outdated? In one way, yes. That does not at all negate, however, the benefit of writing down your feelings and ideas. By writing your feelings and ideas, you will have much clearer insight into how you should pray, meditate upon, and study God's Word. Statements about feelings and ideas are a starting place, not an ending place.

For that matter, a workbook such as this one is not an "answer book"—it is more like a "self-evaluation book." It is a means of helping you reach a particular goal—in this case, finding peace.

## THERE IS NO TEST

So often when we were children, we were given workbooks that accompanied textbooks. Those workbooks were used to reinforce certain facts and ideas—they were intended to help a student focus on the major points of the textbook so the student would be better prepared for a test.

I have good news for you—there's no test associated with this workbook! Rather, this workbook is intended to help you focus on certain ideas and principles from God's Word so you can better understand your relationship with God, who you are as a person, and discover how you might improve your relationship with other people. The things you write in this book are for your benefit, not for the benefit of any other person.

So what should be discussed and what shouldn't be discussed? Look for this symbol and heading:

### DISCUSSION POINT

The questions or ideas that follow this symbol and heading are especially good for personal meditation and reflection and group discussion.

## KEY FEATURE 2:
## A LETTER TO GOD

Many years ago I developed a practice that has proven to be highly valuable to me through countless situations, heartaches, and challenges. I began to write letters to God.

In the beginning I wrote out my letters in longhand, later on a typewriter, and today on my computer. I write just as if I were writing a personal letter to a friend—and in truth, the Lord is the Friend of friends, the best Friend any person will ever have. Jesus invited His disciples to call Him "Friend" and relate to Him as "Friend." He calls us to do the same today. (See John 15:14–15.)

In a letter, I'd pour out my heart to the Lord. At times my letter was filled with statements that were marked by anguish, hurt, or pain. Sometimes my letter was a statement that allowed me to vent very deep frustrations, disappointments, or concerns. Sometimes it would be a place for me to identify questions I had—along with a plea for God's answers. Sometimes my letters were a way for me to tell God about my worries and fears.

Some of my letters were fairly short. Others were very long.

Two of the greatest things about these letters is that they were and continue to be very honest and very personal. There's no point in writing a letter to God if it isn't totally, brutally, and completely honest. Who are you trying to kid? God knows what's lurking in your heart and mind. He knows what is troubling you. The benefit of your expressing yourself so honestly and fully to God is not to inform God about something. The benefit is so you can reread what you have written and inform yourself about what it is that you are truly thinking and feeling.

"Well, then," you may be saying, "why don't you call it a letter to self? Why call it a letter to God?"

Because a letter to God has a spiritual context and it is rooted in your relationship to God. In some ways, it's like the difference between talking to yourself as you drive on the freeway and actually spending time talking aimlessly to God in the quiet of your own living room after everybody else in the house has gone to bed.

Let me give you an example of this by sharing a letter from a young woman who gave me permission to share this with you. I recommended to her that she write a letter to God after she experienced a terrible loss in her life. This is what she later wrote to me:

Dear Dr. Stanley:

I can't tell you how much you helped me when you told me to write a letter to God. I told you that I didn't know why God let my boyfriend Ted die in a car crash just a few weeks before our wedding. I was devastated when Ted died. He was the love of my life and my future. I've never hurt as bad about anything as I did when I got the call that Ted was gone. I thought my life was over—in fact, I hate to admit it, but I was thinking about committing suicide. I just couldn't imagine living without Ted. You told me to pour out all my feelings to God in a letter.

I am not proud of the fact but I'm going to tell you anyway—I thought your idea was dumb. It seemed like a waste of time. But I couldn't get the idea out of my head so I finally decided to do it.

Well, I wrote and wrote, and then I wrote some more. I ended up with thirty-seven pages! I've never written anything that long before, much less a letter. Every time I'd think I was done with the letter, I'd think of something else to say.

When I was done with the letter, I read it all the way through. That was a pretty intense evening. I kept thinking, Did I really say that? Did I really mean that? The answer was "yes" every time. I didn't write down anything I didn't think or feel—no matter how bad it was. I'm sure lots of people would say I wasn't sounding very Christian in some parts of my letter.

In some parts, I was really angry with God. (There are lots of exclamation points in those parts!)

In some parts, I was hurting so bad. There are some places where my tears nearly blotted out the ink so I could barely make out the words—I don't remember crying that hard at the time I was writing but I must have been.

At the end of writing the letter, I was completely wiped out. But that's not a bad thing. When I look back now I realize that I had been saying some of these same things to my family members or friends—or to myself—but in saying these things to other people or in the shower, I never really got to the "end" of what I had to say. I never really got it all out. This time I did. I had one big thirty-seven-page letter of getting it all out.

I put the letter in my Bible and stuck it in a drawer and then I don't know why but I slept and slept and slept—I didn't do much else but sleep for several days. I hadn't been able to sleep very much in the days and weeks after Ted died but after writing that letter to God I was able to sleep. I even called in to my job and took a couple of vacation days just so I could sleep.

Afterward, I felt better. I had a real feeling of calm all the way through my body. I found I could think about things other than Ted. I noticed flowers blooming in the window box of my apartment—they were probably there before but I hadn't seen them. I heard birds singing. They were probably singing before but I hadn't heard them.

I don't really know how to explain this but it was as if my mind had slowed down and I could take in life again. My mind had been spinning and spinning—I saw a movie last week about a woman who went hysterical and I knew how she felt. I hadn't done what she did but I had felt the way she felt deep down inside me. Those feelings weren't there after I finished sleeping. I guess you could say I was more peaceful in my heart.

A friend told me I had finally "accepted" what had happened. I don't think that was it. I think I had just poured out my whole heart to God and in place of all I had poured out, God had poured Himself back into my heart. It was a really good feeling.

About two weeks later, I opened my Bible and there was my letter. I started reading back through it, but I didn't get very far. It was like pulling the scab off a sore that had started to heal. I said to myself, "I don't feel that way anymore." And that's the truth, I don't. I finally put the letter into a locked box of very personal things. I may want to read it again someday—it might help me to get through another sad or awful time, or it might help me to help somebody else someday. But right now, I don't want to read it again. And I don't want any-body else reading it. It's just between me and God, and that's the place it needs to stay.

So, thank you, Dr. Stanley, for teaching me to do this. I probably will write other let-ters to God in the future. I certainly will tell other people who are hurting to do this. There's one thing I know . . . I don't need to write God any more right now about Ted's death. I sent that letter to heaven and heaven sent back a reply. Heaven wrote back in my heart: "Have hope. God has a good future for you."

There are two things I don't want you to miss in this young woman's beautifully written and heartfelt letter.

First, she completely emptied herself of all she was feeling and thinking about this par-ticular hurt or trouble. She held back nothing. There's only so much you can say to friends or family members about certain issues before they tune you out. You probably know that to be true in your heart, even if you've never thought about it before. God alone is able to hear *all* you have to say.

When you talk to other people about a problem—or even to yourself—it's like rehears-ing lines from a play. You engrave your feelings and opinions deeper and deeper on your memory. You never let them go.

In writing out everything to God, you reach the point where you've said it all and you can let it go.

Second, she kept her letter to God personal. That's the only way a letter can be if you truly are going to write down all that you feel or think. God is the only One who will never judge you or put you down for expressing yourself fully and completely, even if you are angry or hateful toward Him. He can take it!

Of all the things that you write into this workbook, your letters to God are likely to be the most personal. Keep these letters private! You'll find a couple of blank pages provided each time I suggest you write a letter to God. You may need more space than that—maybe many more pages. If so, use blank paper of your own and slot those extra pages into the workbook at this point.

One man asked me, "Can I write my letter to God on my computer?"

My answer is "yes." But make sure it isn't your computer at work. And make sure you file it away so that only you are likely to find it. Mark it as a text file with a password that only you can access.

I realize that I have spent a great deal of time on this issue of privacy but it is very important, and especially so because the subject we are dealing with is your peace.

You won't have peace if you think the ideas or feelings you are expressing—and especially those that others might perceive as being negative—are floating around in a way that they can be fired back at you in a mortar shell of criticism or rebuke.

On the other hand, you won't really get to the point where you experience genuine and abiding peace if you don't face some hard issues and questions that *require* you to be completely candid and to express the totality of your feelings.

A letter to God has these two rules:

1. Get it all out before God.

2. Keep it all private from other people.

## WHAT ABOUT SHARING MY LETTER WITH A COUNSELOR?

One person recently asked me, "But what about sharing some of this with a professional counselor?"

What you reveal to a counselor is up to you. Make sure the counselor is truly a person who "watches out for your soul" as a person who feels he or she must give account to God. Make sure what you share is kept in professional confidence. Make sure your counselor is a Christian who truly wants God's eternal best for you.

## KEY FEATURE 3:
## THANKS-AND-PRAISE LISTS

Virtually everything that causes us *not* to feel peace is negative. Let me make a couple of general statements related to that truth.

Peace is positive. Not everything that is positive in this world is peace—not everything that is positive in this world produces peace. But peace is 100 percent positive.

Everything that is negative—whether spiritual, material, emotional, or mental—has the potential for destroying peace. Everybody I know would agree that these situations have a very strong negative slant to them: sickness, mental illness, war, acts of terrorism, divorce, fighting with another person, bankruptcy, losing a job, a runaway child. The root causes of many problems are also mostly negative: rebellion, anger, sin, hate, injustice, rejection, bitterness, fear, anxiety, oppression, and depression. Every one of these things can impact a person's peace.

What can we do to turn ourselves away from a negative situation or condition and toward a positive state of peace?

The first answer many people give is "pray." Actually, the first answer is one type of prayer: thanksgiving and praise.

Thanksgiving focuses on the blessings we have received from God—all of the positive things we have experienced or are experiencing.

Praise focuses us on the Giver of all blessings—it points us toward the attributes and nature of God, which is 100 percent positive all the time!

We are wise, then, when we are troubled, or when we find ourselves in negative or disturbing situations and conditions, to begin to praise and thank God.

From time to time in this workbook I will challenge you to make a *Thanks and Praise* list. Be creative in making your lists. List things that are highly concrete and specific, and things that are abstract and more general. For example, you might thank God for "a family who loves me," "beauty," "the light through my kitchen window," "answers," and "for seeing two beautiful butterflies in my yard." Nothing is too great or too small for thanksgiving!

The same holds true for your praise. So often we repeat the phrase "Praise God" over and over and never mention any aspect of His nature in our praise. Praise God for being your Savior, your Healer, your Deliverer, your Sure Foundation. Praise God for His glory, His majesty, His splendor, His power, His love, His tender care, His leading and guidance, and His willingness to protect and provide.

Both lists could be endless. Make your thanks-and-praise lists as long as you want them. The longer your lists, the more likely you are to find yourself rising up out of the pits of despair, fear, and anxiety and the more likely you are to "find peace."

Two things are sure to happen as you pour out thanksgiving and praise to God:

*First,* your faith will be strengthened. You'll begin to catch a new glimpse of how great God is and how much more powerful He is than any problem you have. You'll catch a glimpse of how much God loves you and desires the best for you.

The God who has given you so much has so much more to give!

The God who has done so much for you through the years isn't finished working in your life.

The God who has been so much bigger than any problem you ever faced in your past is bigger than any problem you have now.

The God who was with you then is with you in this moment.

*Second,* your heart and mind will be opened up in fresh new ways to receive insights into God's Word. You'll catch a glimpse of God's infinite wisdom, which He desires to share with you in generous, overflowing portions. (See James 1:5.)

You will begin to understand with your spirit—not just your mind—that God has an answer for you, a plan for you, a purpose for you, a peace to give to you.

Fear is not God's plan. Neither is worry or anxiety.

Living in conflict in your marriage or in your relationship with your children is not God's plan.

Experiencing plaguing doubts or haunting memories is not part of God's plan.

If these things are not God's plan and purpose for you, what is? This is the question that leads a person to a study of God's Word on very important and often highly personal subjects.

"How does this work?" you may be asking.

Let me give you an example. If you are sick, injured, or in any kind of physical difficulty, you need to begin thanking God for the strength, enduring power, energy, and health He has given you in the past, and you need to begin praising God as your Healer and your Restorer. As you do this, you are going to find that your mind is made very alert to passages in the Bible that refer to healing and that give very practical advice about healing. You are also going to find that various names and attributes of God seem to jump out at you, names such as "the Balm of Gilead" or "the Repairer of the Breech." There are dozens of names of God that depict His attributes of healing and restoration.

You are going to find yourself especially drawn to passages that portray miracles of healing and restoration, or that tell us about God's abiding strength to help a person endure suffering, pain, and affliction.

You will begin to see more of God's purpose in allowing some people to suffer or to experience illness, weakness, or injury. You very likely will gain much wisdom about the blessings and benefits that can come to a person who endures physical difficulties with faith.

Now, when you combine the faith that is built up from your thanksgiving and praise, with the wisdom that begins to rise up from your thanksgiving and praise, you are going to find that you are in a wonderful position to know how to act in all situations with greater confidence, joy, power, and yes . . . peace!

Do not take thanksgiving and praise lightly. The making of these lists can open up something deep within you that is directly linked to your experiencing the presence and power of God.

## KEY FEATURE 4:
## FILING A GRIEVANCE STATEMENT

All of us know what it means to hold a grudge against another person. A grudge is a feeling of resentment, bitterness, anger, or even hatred. Grudges develop when we feel rejected or when we believe we have been treated unfairly or unjustly.

The trouble is, very often we begin to hold a grudge against someone and we don't recognize it as a grudge. We don't own up to our feelings in the moment—rather, we "stuff them" deep inside and allow them to fester there. No matter how completely we think we have stuffed such feelings, they inevitably erupt in the form of an angry outburst, a gripping fear, an overwhelming wave of helplessness, or a spewing out of bitter accusations. What then?

Well, we likely find ourselves in a position where we have hurt others, and in the bigger picture, we have hurt ourselves. We have allowed something very negative to build up inside us—something directly linked to and directly opposite to our finding and experiencing ongoing peace.

Very often when a person goes to a counselor and says, "I just don't have any peace," the counselor will work first to identify the source of what is troubling a person. For example, it might be a recurring nightmare, an ongoing feud, or deep feelings of being angry about abuse that happened early in childhood.

A great deal of this identification work can be done by a person who goes to God with an open heart and says, "Lord, please show me why I don't have peace. Please reveal to me why peace seems to be so elusive."

I truly believe that if you make this request of the Lord and are truly patient in listening for His response—reading His Word faithfully, studying areas of concern more fully—that He will show you what it is that is striking against the peace God desires for you to experience.

In all cases, the thing that is striking against your peace involves a person or a group of people. Problems don't exist in a vacuum. They don't come packaged like a box of cereal. Problems in life are related to people, including the very real person of the devil. In some cases, the person is your own self and the bad behavior that you continually and willfully choose to pursue. In many cases, the person related to your lack of peace is a person you know and, very likely, know well. It may be your spouse, your employer, your father or mother, your child, your friend, or a relative such as a grandparent, aunt, or uncle. It may be a teacher, coach, pastor, or other authority figure in your past or present.

There's something about what that person did or didn't do . . . said or didn't say . . . that has given you a framework so that any one of a number of situations can rise up and assault your peace.

"But my lack of peace began with the 9/11 attack on America," one person told me. "How is that linked to a person?"

One of the first things that happened after the 9/11 attack was this: Those in political authority looked for *who* caused the attack. That's very often what we do when trouble strikes—we look for the person to blame.

Few people in the United States had heard the name Osama bin Laden before September 11, 2001. Today, I doubt if you could find a mentally healthy adult in America who doesn't know that man's name. The foremost person linked to those terrorist attacks that rocked our nation on September 11, 2001, is Osama bin Laden, even though he personally didn't fly the airplanes that were hijacked to create such horrible devastation, not only in the lives and families of tens of thousands, but in the souls of millions.

Osama bin Laden is not the only person associated with a lack of peace experienced in relationship with the 9/11 attacks, however. There are two other "people" directly related to a loss of peace that you feel because of that horrible day of assault on our nation.

First, there's a person somewhere in your past or present who is the main person who has influenced HOW you interpreted what happened on September 11, and how you continue to interpret it. Some people were deeply troubled by the events of 9/11. I was among them. I ached for the people whose lives had been lost and whose loved ones had died. I felt that in some way I had been injured because my nation was injured. There are some people, however, who have never moved beyond the initial shock and horror of September 11, 2001. They still have nightmares. They are still afraid to fly in an airplane. They are still expecting an act of terrorism to strike their lives at any moment of any day. Some still feel tremendous hatred and anger.

What's the difference between a person who is still in deep shock over 9/11 and one who isn't?

The person who was able to grieve over the hurt and pain of 9/11 and be healed of that grief is a person who had been taught certain things about life—how to mourn a loss and then move ahead with faith and optimism, how to let go of hate, how to forgive, how to love, and so forth.

There's someone in your past or present who has been your role model for how to deal with situations and circumstances that are related to worry, anxiety, sin, loss, or anything else that damages your peace. There's someone in your past or present who has taught you how to find peace. In other words, there's someone in your personal history who has taught you how to cope with life—both the good and bad experiences that come to each of us. Even if you do not believe you can identify any one person who has instructed you in how to recover from a loss, get over a hurt, or respond positively to a painful wound—surely the Lord Jesus Christ is such a person. He is our ultimate role model for how to deal with all negative situations.

In addition to the person you may identify as the one who damaged your peace, and the person who has taught you how to recover from a negative situation and regain your peace, is a third person. That person is the enemy of your soul—the one called the devil or Satan in the Bible. He is the person in the shadows behind all manifestations of evil.

Make no mistake about it, the devil is real and he is your *enemy*—at all times, in all situations. He strikes against you to steal from you everything that is valuable to you, destroy your integrity and your reputation, and take your very life. The devil uses people, but he is the force behind the force when it comes to many serious negative blows against your peace.

Some people make a very grave error in blaming God for what is truly the devil's work. I recently read about a man who admits openly that he still holds God accountable for "killing his mother," who died when he was seven years old. He refuses to accept Jesus as his Savior because he is angry with God and is trying to get even with Him for what He supposedly did fifty-five years ago!

I have news for this man—God did not kill his mother. He's believed the wrong thing for more than five decades. God may have allowed the devil to do his dastardly work, but God did not kill his mother. This man needs to turn his anger toward the one who did, the devil. (See John 10:10.)

Furthermore, what is the benefit in being angry with a loving God who desires to heal and restore this painful experience in his life? Who is this man hurting? Only himself! It's time for him—and perhaps for you—to come to grips with the fact that there is an enemy of your soul and he is the one who is out to destroy you in any way he can. Jesus came to give you life—an *abundance* of life, including all things that are for your benefit now and in eternity.

We each face, then, three people as we face a negative situation in our lives:

- a human enemy who has hurt us (willfully or unwittingly)

- a person who has taught us how to cope with life—with both the good and bad experiences of life—or who has failed in some way to teach us how to deal with life's negatives in a positive way

- the spiritual enemy of our souls, the devil

Who is it that we file a grievance against?

It may be one, two, or all three of these people! It's up to you to determine just who you may be holding a grudge against for the pain they've caused you, directly or indirectly. It's up to you to determine how you've been injured by that person, either directly or indirectly. If you have a grievance, which we all have from time to time, it's critically important that you be able to identify every person who is part of that grievance.

## FILING A GRIEVANCE STATEMENT

A grievance statement is a very straightforward statement about what you think a person did to you that hurt you in any way.

Start your grievance statement this way: "I have a grievance against you, _____ _____ (fill in the person's name)."

A grievance statement very often continues with one of these phrases:

"I felt great hurt or pain when you . . ."

"I suffered injury or loss when you . . ."

"I felt deep disappointment when you . . ."

"I am very angry at you for . . ."

"I believe you were very wrong when you . . ."

Please note that you are not starting these phrases with the word *you* but with the word *I*. Also note that you are acknowledging your own emotional response to what a person may have done.

Some people blast others with a "You did this" or "You said that" or "You caused" attitude or statement. While it may be true that the other person did, said, or caused exactly what you identify, it may also be true that the other person had no idea what they were really doing, saying, or causing! The only aspect of what happened that is 100 percent knowable on your part is how you felt in response to what another person did.

In this part of the grievance statement you need to list everything that comes to mind.

I know a man whose wife divorced him, and he ended up writing down a full account of more than thirty conversations or experiences in which he had felt deeply wounded by what his former wife had done or said *before* the divorce.

A while later, he wrote out a grievance statement in which he documented more than a dozen experiences in which he felt anguish or pain as the result of what his wife had done or said *during* the divorce proceedings.

One woman told me she wrote out a grievance statement against her father, who had abused her as a child. She wrote out ten experiences. Six months later she went back and wrote out ten more. This went on for several years. In all, she believes that she documented in her grievance statements more than a hundred grievances she was holding against her father.

Neither this man nor this woman had even started dealing with the devil or with the person who had taught them how to cope—or how not to cope—with life's problems.

In the case of the man who went through a divorce, I suspect that he hasn't even thought about addressing the fact that nobody had taught him how to deal with some of the negative and hurtful behavior of his wife early on in his marriage. In the case of the woman who had been abused, I suspect that she hasn't even acknowledged that the devil was pulling the strings of her father's behavior.

## WHY IS A GRIEVANCE STATEMENT SO IMPORTANT?

These statements are a way of bringing to the surface the pain and hurt that are festering deep inside your soul.

It is a way of flushing out bitterness and resentment. It is a way of bringing wounds to the surface so they can be cleansed and healed.

The point is not simply to write out a grievance statement, but then to submit that statement to the Lord Jesus.

It is to hold this statement before the Lord and say, "Jesus, You see how I feel. You see what this person did to me. You see how my life has been impacted by this and how much anguish I've been living with. I give this grievance statement to You. Please deal with this person who has trespassed on my life and caused me offense. Please deal with me too—heal me, restore me, help me to move from pain to wholeness, from weakness to strength, from shame to forgiveness. The weight of these memories is holding me down. Please free me from these memories so I might hold my head high and walk forward into my future with boldness, strength, and renewed energy. Please cleanse me fully by the power of Your Holy Spirit."

Is there scriptural support for doing this? Yes. There are a number of times in the Bible when men and women "reminded" God of what had happened to them in the past. The psalmist, especially, cries out to God on repeated occasions to tell God what his enemies have done to him and how he has been hurt by them. But . . . the psalmist does not live with despair. In nearly all cases, the psalmist makes a strong declaration of God's strength and delivering power.

Psalm 57 is one example of this:

> My soul is among lions;
> I lie among the sons of men
> Who are set on fire,
> Whose teeth are spears and arrows,
> And their tongue a sharp sword.
> Be exalted, O God, above the heavens;
> Let Your glory be above all the earth.
> They have prepared a net for my steps;
> My soul is bowed down;
> They have dug a pit before me;
> Into the midst of it they themselves have fallen.
> My heart is steadfast, O God, my heart is steadfast;
> I will sing and give praise.
> Awake, my glory!
> Awake, lute and harp!
> I will awaken the dawn.
> I will praise You, O Lord, among the peoples;
> I will sing to You among the nations.
> For Your mercy reaches unto the heavens,
> And Your truth unto the clouds. (Ps. 57:4–10)

In these seven verses, the psalmist makes a major grievance statement citing very specific wrongs that have been done against him and expressing very clearly his strong feelings. He also declares the glory and mercy of God "above all the earth!"

## SUBMITTING A GRIEVANCE STATEMENT TO THE LORD

In submitting a grievance statement to the Lord, I strongly suggest that you get down on your knees before the Lord. Hold your grievance statement in your hands and pray as I suggested, and then begin to declare the power and goodness of God over each aspect of your grievance statement.

For example, if someone ridiculed you in the presence of your children, declare that the Lord can turn this from evil to good. Ask the Lord to blot all remembrance of this incident from your children's minds and hearts.

If someone spoke lies about you, declare that the Lord is the Author of all truth. Ask the Lord to let the truth prevail.

If someone has rejected you, declare God's great love, forgiveness, and acceptance of you. Ask the Lord to heal your broken heart and to reassure you of His everlasting love for you.

Several years ago I went through an extremely painful emotional experience in my own life. One of the things that helped me most was writing a statement of grievances. I listed all of the wrongs that I felt had been committed against me. It took me several hours to do this. I wrote down all of the things that I had been mulling over in my mind—you know, the types of things that keep you awake at night and keep coming back around to torment you. My list was a fairly long list. As I read back through it, I felt all the emotions you might expect—anger, frustration, sorrow.

But then, when I took that list to the Lord and handed it over to Him, I felt great release. I felt in my heart, *That's it. No more thinking about those negative things. No more raw pain and no more anger. It's all in God's hands. If He wants to think about these matters, fine, but I'm finished thinking about them.*

## THIS IS YOUR WORKBOOK

If you see this workbook as something you are going to accomplish—as something that is going to be truly helpful to you—something that can change the way you feel and think from the inside out and enable you to experience the comforting and abiding peace of God in your life, then you will reap great benefit.

# About the Author

D R. CHARLES F. STANLEY is founder and president of In Touch Ministries, whose *In Touch* radio and television ministry is broadcast around the world in thirty-three languages. He has also been the senior pastor of the 15,000-member First Baptist Church in Atlanta, Georgia, for more than thirty years.

Dr. Stanley received his bachelor of arts degree from the University of Richmond, his bachelor of divinity degree from Southwestern Theological Seminary, and his master's and doctor's degrees from Luther Rice Seminary. He has twice been elected president of the Southern Baptist Convention and is the author of many books, including *Finding Peace, God Is in Control, Seeking His Face, Walking Wisely, When Tragedy Strikes, The Source of My Strength, Success God's Way,* and *How to Listen to God.*